THE **Kids & Consent** CURRICULUM

25

Whole-Classroom Lessons
to Teach Boundaries,
Collaboration,
and Respect

SARAH CASPER
Consent Educator | @comprehensiveconsent

THE KIDS AND CONSENT CURRICULUM

Published by
PESI Publishing, Inc.
3839 White Ave
Eau Claire, WI 54703

Cover and interior design by Emily Dyer
Editing by Jenessa Jackson, PhD

ISBN 9781683737872 (print)
ISBN 9781683737889 (ePUB)
ISBN 9781683737896 (ePDF)

PESI Publishing
pesipublishing.com

Table of Contents

Introduction

Welcome to *The Kids and Consent Curriculum.* My name is Sarah (it's pronounced like SAH-rah). My pronouns are she/her. I'm a former PsyD candidate turned consent educator, here to help you give your students the mindfulness, decision-making, and social-emotional learning (SEL) skills that they need to navigate boundaries and desires and create healthy relationships.

Why I Wrote This Book

Ever since the #MeToo movement, founded by organizer Tarana Burke, gained traction in late 2017, awareness of the importance of consent has increased. However, there are limited resources aimed at helping kids, tweens, and teens develop the interpersonal skills to support them in their consent practices—in navigating boundaries and desires with respect. In elementary and middle school, if students learn about consent, it's usually in the context of "unsafe touch" (that is, child sexual abuse prevention). It's not until high school or college that students are taught to explore and consider normative interactions when it comes to healthy relationships and personal boundaries. Even then, these lessons are deprioritized and lack the scaffolding, self-reflection, coaching, and repetition required for students to successfully internalize the knowledge and call on their skills.

But we don't need to wait until children are adolescents to engage them in learning to practice consent. On the contrary, it is arguably dangerous to wait. Without consent education, children will likely pick up behaviors that contradict the exact values we plan to teach them later in life. Consider the images, music, TV shows, movies, and so on that our young people absorb daily. Our culture sends the message that men pushing women up against walls and kissing them is "romantic." That girls and women who say no are "teases" and "prudes." We shouldn't be surprised by the frequency of sexual violence and relational harm. This is what's being modeled in the mainstream media, which means that by the time students are in their teens, inadequate behavioral patterns may already have been established. If high school is the first time that a school is providing consent education, students will have to unlearn old patterns *as* they try to learn new ones.

This is where this curriculum comes in. We know that if we want students to have strong skills in areas such as mathematics, reading, and writing, we need to strategically engage them in learning and practice. As research in the field of SEL shows, the same is true for having strong relationship skills. This curriculum is designed with this in mind. It gives professionals like yourself a practical way to help students ages 8 to 13 navigate their own boundaries and desires alongside the boundaries and desires of others. Although it was primarily written as a resource for educators to use in their classrooms, it is also applicable for psychologists, social workers, childcare workers, and parents who want to help kids and tweens develop the skills needed to support healthy relationships. Since this is an SEL curriculum, it can be introduced alongside other SEL practices too.

What This Book *Is*

This book contains research-informed and skills-based lessons to teach students how to navigate boundaries and desires and practice consent when the stakes are low so they're prepared when the stakes are high.

Telling students what consent *is* isn't enough to create behavioral changes. If we want to increase children's ability to practice consent in their teenage and adult years, we must provide programming that allows them to develop the skills needed to navigate consent and boundaries, engages them in critical reflection, provides them a space to discuss their own experiences, and builds their skills for engaging in communication differences (Hirsch et al., 2019; Lockwood Harris, 2018; Pound et al., 2017; Setty, 2020). This curriculum puts these recommendations into actionable lesson plans. It goes beyond outlining what consent is and isn't. It supports students in recognizing and overcoming the barriers to practicing consent (on all sides of an encounter) and supports teachers in creating environments that uphold the values promoted in each lesson.

Even though this book isn't *about* sex, it *is* a sexual violence prevention tool. While sexual violence can be perpetrated intentionally and maliciously, it can also be perpetrated by young people who—lacking other models and education—learned about relationships and sex through a culture that reinforces gender norms and by watching mainstream media and pornography. Teenagers and young adults follow the social scripts they've been passively building for years. By helping kids build consent skills and internalize the values of autonomy and respect at a young age, we give them alternative social scripts to the ones they see on their screens. We give them the tools for making safer and kinder choices for themselves and for others. In separating the practice of consent from the world of sex, as these lessons do, we can teach kids at a young age how to notice what they want, ask for permission, recognize their limits, advocate for their boundaries, handle rejection with grace, and be accountable when they misstep. Helping kids develop these skills now gives them opportunities to practice and establish healthier ways of relating that will support them in their friendships now and in their intimate relationships in the future.

What This Book *Isn't*

While this is a curriculum about kids and consent, it's neither a legal resource nor a child sexual abuse prevention tool. Child sexual abuse prevention focuses on the sexual violence that can be perpetrated by older predators against children. This book helps kids and tweens develop the SEL skills needed to navigate consent on all sides of an encounter. While it *indirectly* supports abuse prevention efforts, it primarily focuses on building skills that support kids in practicing consent within their normative friendships and sibling relationships. Adults who work with or care for youth must be able to help children learn how to create respectful relationships *and* how to help prevent child sexual abuse. Please see the appendix for child sexual abuse prevention resources.

Because this book is not a legal resource, but an SEL resource, its focus is on *practicing* consent, rather than giving and getting consent. "Giving consent" and "getting consent" is the language of policy and the law. In legal proceedings, where the only options are guilty or not guilty, a judge and jury have to know where the line is so that they can determine whether it was crossed—was valid permission given or was it not? In classrooms, where students are navigating the nuances of friendships, our job is to be not arbiters of right and wrong but teachers of ideas and skills. We have an opportunity to introduce consent as an ongoing practice of relating that's rooted in the values of choice, mutuality, care, and respect. In our everyday lives, we can scrap the transactional language of "giving" and "getting" and, instead, use language that reflects the dynamic experience of navigating relationships in a way that values the desires and boundaries of everyone involved. This curriculum intentionally uses the language of *practicing consent* for this reason.

What's Inside

This curriculum is divided into six modules, each focused on a specific set of skills. Across the modules you'll find a total of 25 lesson plans full of skill-building activities and discussion questions to help students grapple with complex and nuanced ideas surrounding consent.

Each lesson plan contains information on the objectives, materials needed, instructions, and time needed to complete each lesson. Lessons are 15 to 60 minutes long. If necessary, you can facilitate any of the lessons over multiple days. At the end of each lesson, there are guides for supporting consent culture in your classroom and any worksheets, skit scripts, or other handouts you might need.

Module 1: Laying the Groundwork introduces students to the concept of consent, decision-making rights, and the process of practicing consent. The lessons in this module are fundamental. There can be no single step-by-step guide to practicing consent well because no two scenarios are the same and because our desires and boundaries are dynamic. This module helps students understand how this idea is reflected in the concept of practicing consent and helps them internalize the idea that a consent practice is key to healthy relationships.

Module 2: I Ask for What I Want takes students through the journey of recognizing their wants and communicating them with others. The lessons in this module review how students can tune into their bodies to gather information about their desires, how to use that information to make decisions, how to make clear requests with kindness for themselves and others, the social and emotional barriers to making requests, and the consequences of operating under assumptions. By addressing these skills first, we are reminding students that the practice of consent starts with a recognition of their wants and others' rights. We break from the idea that consent is something another person gives or doesn't give and, instead, reinforce the idea that consent is a practice of communicating your desires and boundaries and learning about other people's desires and boundaries.

Module 3: I Listen to Their Response gives students the tools for interpreting someone's response and responding to that response. Communication happens verbally and nonverbally, through word choice and body language. In this module, students will learn the importance of, and the skills for, incorporating another person's full response when they suggest an activity, make a request, or extend an invitation. They will explore the nuances of body language, yeses, noes, maybes, and collaboration. Students will gain practical experience in receiving a no, in responding to a no with grace, and in collaborating on a decision that accounts for both individuals' perspectives.

Module 4: I Share My Limits prepares students to recognize and communicate their limits when they are on the receiving side of a request, suggestion, or invitation. Students will build on their ability to notice their bodies and explore how they can use what they notice to set assertive boundaries when an activity is first proposed or a request is first made, as well as during an ongoing interaction. Within these lessons, students will discuss the various challenges to saying "No" or "Stop," build compassion for themselves when saying no feels impossible, and discover strategies they can use to overcome obstacles to setting boundaries.

Module 5: I Do My Part in Caring for the Both of Us helps students recognize that even when we know *how* to practice consent, we might make mistakes. Others will cross our boundaries, and we will cross others' boundaries. This module helps students identify where their skills can be improved, recognize the difference between pressure and negotiation, understand what tools they can call upon when others make mistakes, and develop the skills to be accountable when they have erred.

Module 6: Wrap-up gives students an opportunity to reflect on their learning journey, celebrate themselves for all the work they've done, and plan for how they will keep practicing.

How to Use This Book

The following are the best practices for delivering these lessons:

1. **Lessons are best presented in the order in which they are written.** While the lessons can be delivered according to need, it's recommended that you follow the order in which the curriculum is written. At the very least, I encourage you to begin with the lessons in module 1.

2. **Use in groups or one-on-one.** The lessons in this book are written to be delivered in a classroom or group setting. With slight adjustments, however, the activities can be made relevant for one-on-one learning.

3. **Adjust according to student need.** The curriculum is written for kids and tweens ages 8 to 13. Adjust your delivery, language, and examples to provide the most developmentally appropriate lessons to your students. Scripts are provided within each lesson. Please improvise as needed. Often, students themselves will come up with fun and meaningful ways to alter the activities. Supporting the self-generated excitement of the students can help them better retain the information and make it resonate for them.

4. **Review the lessons ahead of time.** By visiting the material beforehand, you'll come to each lesson prepared with the necessary mindset and materials. This will also give you time and space to make adjustments as you see fit.

5. **Use your judgment when it comes to timing.** Decide which questions to spend the most time on and how many students to engage in each discussion. Do your best to balance your goals with student goals, keeping in mind both the power of student-led discussion and the importance of the lesson's objectives.

6. **Be vulnerable.** Talking about relationships, feelings, desires, and boundaries is vulnerable stuff! Consider what *you* can share within these lessons to model what an answer might look like and to demonstrate that vulnerability can be scary but there is value in sharing your perspective and experiences.

7. **Be curious.** When you notice yourself feeling apprehensive in response to a student's answer, reflect their statement back to them to make sure you understood it. If appropriate, help them consider the assumptions at the core of their idea. Encourage them to empathize with other perspectives. This curriculum is all about the ways that curiosity can help us better understand ourselves and each other. Exploring students' good-faith responses will often elicit rich perspective and conversation for the entire group.

8. **Repeat the activities and reinforce the lessons.** Skill-building takes time. Repeat the activities and exercises. Reinforce the principles you explore outside of the structured lesson. Read and review the *Supporting This Lesson in Your Classroom's Culture* guide at the end of each lesson. Pay attention when a child is having trouble navigating the interplay of desires and boundaries, refer back to the lessons, and coach them in figuring out what to do next. Developing usable skills requires practice, and the most powerful practice opportunities will be found in everyday moments within your classroom.

9. **Consider your relationship with this material.** Take the time to consider your relationship with choice, desire, and boundaries as you move through this curriculum with your students. Reflecting on these concepts will improve your ability to model and reinforce the values and skills you're teaching. When it comes to any practice, including consent, there's always more to learn.

10. **Consider the culture of your classroom.** As you facilitate these lessons, pay close attention to ways your classroom culture supports or undermines consent values. I can't stress enough how

important the *Supporting This Lesson in Your Classroom's Culture* section at the end of each lesson will be to making the skills and values you are teaching stick. In module 1, this section provides guidance on solidifying students' understanding of new terminology and core ideas. In modules 2 through 5, this section provides guidance on how to model the skills yourself (*Model It*) and how to coach students in using the skills when they could use the support (*Coach It*).

Engaging Parents and Caregivers

Families that understand and value consent as a collection of SEL skills are invaluable allies in helping children integrate these lessons. To best help students develop their consent skills (and to avoid confusion about what's being taught in a curriculum about consent), connect with parents and caregivers about the learning plan and the learning. Share what consent means for this age group and invite parents and caregivers into learning the skills and strategies for reinforcing consent practices in the home. If you can, prepare a learning session for parents and caregivers to introduce them to the way you'll be talking about consent in your classroom. Demonstrate how these lessons impact your choices in the classroom and how they make consent-aligned choices at home.

In one-on-one conversations with caregivers, you can also discuss the specific skills that have been challenging for the child and collaborate on a plan to support the child as a team. While we are all social learners, children's brains are especially prone to picking up on the habits and behaviors of those around them. Getting the adults in students' lives to understand, value, and commit to reinforcing consent practices is one of the most valuable ways to help a child strengthen the skills they're developing through this learning.

As you begin your journey through this book, remember that your goal is to guide young people in noticing what they want, advocating for themselves, setting boundaries, handling rejection, navigating power dynamics, reflecting on their actions, and so much more. With practice, you can help develop your students' SEL consent skills and, in turn, support them in becoming more self-aware, empathetic, and respectful human beings.

MODULE 1

....

Laying the
Groundwork

Introduction to Consent

Learning Objectives:

By the end of this lesson, students will be able to:

1. Define *consent*.

2. Describe the difference between "getting consent" and "practicing consent."

3. Demonstrate why practicing consent is an important part of maintaining healthy relationships.

4. Demonstrate an understanding of how they already practice consent in their everyday lives

Time: 40 minutes

Materials:

- A copy of *The Giving Tree*, by Shel Silverstein (1964), or means for screening a video of the book (available here https://www.youtube.com/watch?v=XFQZfeHq9wo)

- Worksheet 1.1.1

- Whiteboard

- Whiteboard markers

Before You Start:

- Read through the lesson plan.

- Decide how you will present *The Giving Tree*, by Shel Silverstein, to the class. Acquire a copy of the book or pull up the video link, accordingly.

- Print worksheet 1.1.1 (one per student).

Step 1   Introduce the Curriculum

Guide the class in taking two deep breaths.

"Today is the first day of a new learning journey. We're going to spend time in our classroom thinking about and exploring how to have healthy relationships with others and with ourselves."

Ask the class to share some words or phrases that describe a strong and healthy relationship. Write their answers on the board. Answers may include: caring, thoughtful, kind, respectful, nice, thinking about the other person, sharing, not being selfish, and so on.

"You got it! These are the kinds of relationships we feel good in. But creating these kinds of relationships isn't always easy. By a show of hands, have you ever experienced someone who loves you being somewhat unkind to you—maybe yelling at you, being pushy, or taking something of yours without asking?"

As students respond, share that you have also experienced these moments.

Then, ask, "By a show of hands, have you ever been somewhat unkind to someone you love—maybe yelling at them, being pushy, or taking something of theirs without asking?"

As students respond, share that you have also done these things.

"We often want to be kind and caring friends or siblings, but sometimes it can be hard. It can be challenging to know what the right choice is, and it can be challenging to make that choice. What do you do when a friend wants to play one thing but you want to play something else? What do you do when your sibling is frustrating you but you know that yelling at them or hitting them is unkind? What can you do if you made a promise to classmate, but now you're having a change of heart? What can you do if someone asks you to do something but you don't feel comfortable saying no?

"These are the kinds of questions we will answer along this journey together. We're going to learn how to interact with each other, communicate (or talk to each other), and make decisions in a way that is both respectful and caring to others and to ourselves. We're going learn how to practice consent."

Step 2   Story + Discussion

Write the words *How to practice consent* on the board.

Ask students if they know what *consent* means.

After they respond, say, "The word *consent* often refers to 'permission' or 'agreement.' You might hear someone say, 'You didn't ask for consent for a hug'—meaning, 'You didn't ask for permission for a hug.' Or you might hear someone say, 'That wasn't consensual'—meaning, 'I didn't agree to that.'"

Ask students why permission and agreement are an important part of a healthy relationship.

After they respond, say, "If a friend takes your game without your permission, you probably wouldn't feel like they respected or cared about you. If you jump onto your friend's back even though you agreed not to, they probably wouldn't feel like you respected or cared about them. Permission and agreement help friends understand what's okay and not okay. But agreement and permission aren't always so simple."

Read the book *The Giving Tree*, by Shel Silverstein, to the class. Alternatively, you can watch a read-aloud of this book on YouTube (https://www.youtube.com/watch?v=XFQZfeHq9wo).

DISCUSSION QUESTIONS:

- Thinking about the meaning of consent we just discussed, did the boy in *The Giving Tree* get consent when he took apples and branches from the tree?
  - *Talking points:* In the beginning, it's not clear if the boy and the tree talked about whether he had permission to swing on her branches, eat apples, and so forth, but in the second half of the book, the tree and the boy came to an agreement about what he would take. The boy got consent.

- How do you think the tree felt when the boy grew up and started asking for so much?
  - *Talking points:* Sometimes the tree was described as lonely, sometimes, happy, and sometimes she was "happy . . . but not really" (Silverstein, 1964).

- Throughout the story, what do you think the tree wanted?
  - *Talking points:* For the boy to be happy and also to have a relationship with the boy.

- Do you think the tree realized that she wasn't being upfront or clear about what she wanted?
  - *Talking points:* It's hard to know. Maybe, maybe not. She might have thought the boy would just figure it out.

- Do you think the boy realized that the tree was sad because of his actions?
  - *Talking points:* It's hard to know. Maybe, maybe not. He might have thought that the tree would say something about her sadness or wants if she was sad or wanted something.

"Did the boy do something wrong by asking for so much? Did the tree do something wrong by always making offers? Can we blame the boy for taking the tree's resources when the tree agreed to give so much and even made offers? Can we blame the tree for being sad when the boy said he loved her (carving their initials in a heart), but then ignored her for years at a time? These are complicated questions. They show us that hearing a yes, having permission or agreement, doesn't always mean that everything is okay and that the relationship is healthy and feels good.

"Now you might be wondering, *Why are we going to spend time learning about consent if it's not so helpful?* Well, we're not going to learn about *getting* consent. We're going to learn about *practicing* consent. Practicing consent goes beyond making sure that you have permission; it means putting in the effort to consider yourself and the other person when making decisions that impact both of you. It means giving space for what you want, what you're okay with, and what you're not okay with, *and* giving space for what the other person wants, what they're okay with, and what they're not okay with."

Step 3 Discussion

Refer back to the concept of practicing consent and ask students what it means "to practice."

After they respond, say, "To practice means to do an activity in order to improve or keep up your abilities. Think about what it means to practice playing piano. You get better at playing piano by actually playing piano and repeating certain drills and exercises. If you have a strong piano-playing practice, it means that you are regularly doing those things to keep up with and improve your skills.

"Most of you are pretty familiar with this idea of practice. But how can you practice something that isn't an activity, an instrument, or a sport? How can you practice something like consent, respect, kindness, or care?"

After students respond, offer the following analogy: "We can think of consent as a practice, just like we can think of kindness as a practice. If I want to talk to you and I say, 'Can we please talk?' I am being kind by saying please. But I don't get to just label that entire interaction as kind. Practicing kindness means it's ongoing. We do the things that we know are part of a kindness practice (putting effort into listening, not interrupting, and being thoughtful about our words, our volume, and so forth), we consider how we feel, and we gather information about how the other person feels.

"Now, if I accidentally raise my voice during this conversation with you, it doesn't mean I am an unkind or mean person. You might not even leave the interaction feeling like it was unkind. If I raise my voice and yell at you, it means I made a mistake in my kindness practice. I can apologize, be accountable, and reset. Kindness, like consent, is an ongoing practice. We work to pay attention to ourselves and to the other person and make decisions that are consistent with consent as much as possible."

"Next time we'll dive deeper into learning what a consent practice looks like. For now, let's consider how you might already be practicing consent without even realizing it. Remember, our current definition says that practicing consent goes beyond making sure that you have permission; it means considering yourself *and* the other person when making decisions that impact both of you. It means giving space for what you want, what you're okay with, and what you're not okay with, *and* giving space for what the other person wants, what they're okay with, and what they're not okay with."

Introduce worksheet 1.1.1 to the class and review the instructions. Tell students that throughout these lessons, they will not be required to hand in or share the information on any of the worksheets they complete. Give students about five minutes to complete the questions. Then ask students what they came up with (reminding them not to name names).

Supporting This Lesson in Your Classroom's Culture

- Be careful about using the phrases *give consent* and *get consent*.

  We *practice* consent. If we want kids to internalize consent as an ongoing practice based on mutuality, our language needs to reflect this. Practicing consent means asking first, but it also means paying attention to body language, power dynamics, and the ongoing interaction. When we say "giving consent" and "getting consent" in children's normative interactions, we reduce consent to a limited transaction.

  When you mean permission, say "permission." When one student hugs another student without asking, talk about giving and getting *permission* to help the students recognize why that wasn't okay. Oftentimes, teachers and parents tell their students and children that they didn't "get consent" for a hug in an effort to reinforce the importance of consent. But this confuses the legal concepts of getting and giving consent for specific touch with the everyday concept of getting and giving permission to borrow someone's toys, come into their home, or give them a hug (which is one piece of a consent practice). Using familiar language like giving and getting *permission* will help students apply the value of consent without reducing this life practice to the acquisition of a single yes.

Worksheet 1.1.1

Directions: Reflect on how you already practice consent. Read the definition of *practicing consent* below and answer the questions in the space provided.

We have defined *practicing consent* as going beyond making sure that you have permission; it means putting in the effort to consider yourself and the other person when making decisions that impact both of you. It means giving space for what you want, what you're okay with, and what you're not okay with, *and* giving space for what the other person wants, what they're okay with, and what they're not okay with.

Hint: Think about *The Giving Tree*. What did the tree do well? What did the boy do well? What could they have done better?

1. What do you already do (and not do) in your friendships to make space for what you want and for what the other person wants?

2. What do you already do (and not do) in your friendships to help you be honest about what you're not okay with and to help the other person to be honest about what they're not okay with?

Decision-Making Rights and Bodily Autonomy

Time:
40 minutes

Learning Objectives:

By the end of this lesson, students will be able to:

1. Demonstrate an understanding of the relationship between ownership and permission.

2. Define *bodily autonomy*.

3. Demonstrate an understanding of the limits of bodily autonomy.

4. Describe the choices and limitations of their bodily autonomy in the classroom and at home.

Materials:

- Script 1.2.1
- Worksheet 1.2.1
- Whiteboard
- Whiteboard markers

Before You Start:

- Read through the lesson plan.
- Print script 1.2.1 (two copies).
- Print worksheet 1.2.1 (one copy per student).

Step 1   Introduce the Topic

Guide the class in taking two deep breaths.

"In our last lesson, we started learning about the topic of practicing consent. Practicing consent isn't just about making sure you have permission; it means you put in the effort to consider yourself and the other person when making decisions that impact both of you. It is about giving space for what you want, what you're okay with, and what you're not okay with, *and* giving space for what the other person wants, what they're okay with, and what they're not okay with.

"But the fact that we all have different things that we want, that we're okay with, and that we're not okay with can make practicing consent a big challenge. Imagine I told you that we're going to watch a movie in class, but you all had to agree on the movie. Some of you might be in agreement, but others wouldn't. What happens if the class is split? Who gets to decide? What happens if every student except one agrees, but the reason they don't agree is because they've seen the movie before and it gives them nightmares? What happens if the movie selected by the majority of students is one that *I* don't think is appropriate?

"Even between just two people, disagreement will come up. It's not easy to figure out how to make decisions that recognize everyone when people are so unique and often have different feelings, opinions, likes, wants, and limits. There are many possible solutions in moments like these. But before we get to possible solutions, let's get a better understanding of who gets to make decisions and why."

Step 2   Skit + Discussion

Invite a student to volunteer to perform a short skit with you. If no students are interested in volunteering, ask another teacher to play the student role. Hand the volunteer a copy of script 1.2.1.

Set the scene for the class. Say, "[student's name] is home doing homework at their house when, all of a sudden, I walk in."

Perform the skit. At the end, begin a round of applause, thank the student for participating, and ask them to return to their seat.

DISCUSSION QUESTIONS:

- What decisions did I make in this scene?
  - *Talking points:* You decided to walk into the student's house without asking, to leave your shoes on, to ignore the student's request, to insist that because you're the teacher you get to do whatever you want, and so on.
- Was it okay that I made these decisions? Why or why not?
  - *Talking points:* No. A person doesn't have the right to just come into someone else's house. You were only focused on what you wanted, not on what the other person wanted or was okay with.

- What decisions did the student make?
  - *Talking points:* They decided to speak up when you walked in, to request you take your shoes off, to stand up for their right to choose what happens in their house, and so on.

- Was it okay that they made these decisions? Why or why not?
  - *Talking points:* Yes. They have the right to choose who goes into their house, to ask someone to be respectful about whether they're tracking mud inside, and so on.

Summarize what you hear students say. You might say something like "It sounds like because the student's house is theirs, I can't just decide to barge in and treat it the way I want to treat it. I need permission to do the things I want to do."

Then present another scenario. Say, "Now imagine a scenario where I'm walking by a house and I hear someone inside yelling for help. Then I hear nothing. Is it okay for me to go in to try to help without specific permission to enter?"

As students answer, reinforce that this scenario makes things more complicated because while it's still not your house, we can understand why it might be okay, or even important, to barge in. Some people will still say that it's not okay. Either way, we start to see the importance of getting permission first and the importance of recognizing that permission might not always be the priority.

Present another scenario. Say, "Now imagine a scenario where I'm at someone's house (this time, invited) and they have a no-shoes rule. The problem is that I need to wear shoes because I have a foot condition and I'm in pain without them. We've discussed that the person whose house it is gets to decide what happens in their house, so does that mean I have to just suck it up, take off my shoes, and be in pain?"

As students answer, reinforce that this makes things more complicated because the house belongs to someone else, but your body belongs to you, so you should be able to make decisions about it. You're now in a situation where two people have legitimate claims over the decision. There are certainly compromises and collaborative solutions that can be made. *And* the answer isn't as simple as "It belongs to them, so they get to decide"—because the house belongs to one person and the body to another.

Conclude this section by saying, "We have the right to make decisions about the things that are ours, and sometimes your right to make a decision might not be the priority. In the first scenario, concerns about the other person's health and safety complicated things. In the second scenario, people having different claims (or rights) to different elements complicated things. It wouldn't be okay for me just to decide to wear my shoes, because it is *their* house. It also wouldn't be okay for them to just decide I have to take my shoes off, because they're *my* feet.

"We're going to explore how to make sense of both kinds of scenarios. We're going to explore who gets to be the decider in situations like the first one, where the question is about balancing our right to the things that belong to us with the priority of health and safety. We're also going to start exploring who gets to be the decider in situations similar to the second scenario, where the question is about how people with differing wants, limits, perspectives, and rights can work together so that they communicate and make decisions where both people are respected. This is what most of our future lessons will focus on too."

Step 3   Discussion

Say, "In thinking about things that are ours, the body is a big one. Throughout your life, you might give away your old clothes as hand-me-downs, you might donate toys you no longer use, and you might even move to a new home. But no matter what, your body is always with you and always yours. You get to choose what happens with your body. That means if you don't want someone to hug you (or your body), you get to say no."

Ask the class what decisions they've made about their bodies today. Share a couple of decisions you've made today to get them started (e.g., your hairstyle, your breakfast, the song you listened to in the car, the way you're sitting or standing right now).

Ask the class if there is anyone else who made decisions about their bodies today. Offer some examples (e.g., "Maybe you didn't get to pick your breakfast, or maybe you only had a few options." "Maybe you didn't want to brush your teeth, but your adult said you had to.")

Say, "Everyone has body rights, or bodily autonomy. *Bodily autonomy* means that your body is yours, so you get to make decisions about your body. Your friends, your teachers, and your parents and caregivers all have bodily autonomy, or the right to make choices about their bodies.

"However, as we talked about in the 'no shoes in the house' scenario, there are times when you, alone, might not get to decide what your body does because other people have body rights too. This is something you, in some way, are already familiar with. You know to use an indoor voice when you're inside because if your voice is too loud, it can disturb others. Even though your body is yours, you don't get to yell just because that's what your body wants to do. That's because yelling and being loud impact the others in the room.

"There are also times when bodily autonomy might be put on pause to keep your body healthy and safe. This is something you, in some way, are already familiar with too. We talked about it in the example of someone calling for help, and that you might decide to enter their home even though it doesn't belong to you and you don't have clear permission to enter. You are also probably familiar with this from your own lives. Your adults have certainly told you that you need to wear a seat belt in the car. Even though your body is yours, in health and safety matters like this, your adult must be a big part of the decision."

Step 4 Activity

"Now that we have a better understanding of bodily autonomy, we're going to take time to think about what respecting bodily autonomy, or body rights, looks like in *our* classroom."

Create two columns on the classroom whiteboard. Label one "Decisions That Students Mostly Get to Make on Their Own" and the other "Decisions That Teachers Are a Big Part Of."

Then, one by one, read through each decision on the Decision List below.

DECISION LIST:

- What seat you sit in
- What you wear to school
- Who to play with at recess
- How you sit in your seat
- Whether you wear a jacket outside during recess
- What time lunch starts
- Whether you hug a classmate
- What book you read during reading time
- How much you eat at lunch

Pause after each decision to ask the class whether they think that decision is one that a student gets to make mostly on their own or one that the teacher is a big part of. As students categorize the decisions, write them down on the whiteboard in their respective columns.

Adjust the Decision List as needed based on your specific classroom. Put some answers in the middle. Hear what the students have to say, and talk through why certain decisions are the way they are. Consider whether it's a health and safety issue or a matter of something being a decision that impacts others or that might bump up against a right that someone else has.

It's okay if you and your students have a hard time figuring out how to classify some of these decisions. The goals here are to explore the nuance and to talk about where students have more choice, where they have less choice, and why things are the way they are. For example, "How you sit in your seat" might bring up a conversation about what options students do have and about the need to be respectful of classmates' personal space and learning needs. You also might notice that you can be flexible in giving students more rights. This activity can support the creation of general class guidelines too.

Conclude this section by saying, "When there's a question of health and safety, the adults in your life will sometimes need to be the final decision-makers. We hope that they will include you in the decision-making process, and sometimes they do need to have final say.

"When there's a decision that impacts you and someone else—for example, maybe you want to play a game with a friend, wrestle with a sibling, put loud music on in a shared space—the people who will be impacted by that choice have the right to have a say in the decision. If they don't want to play a game with you, you don't get to make them play the game. If you don't want a piggyback ride, they don't get to make you hop on. Both people need to find a way to work together so that both people are cared for and respected in their friendships."

CLASSROOM MANAGEMENT TIP:

At this point, you might have one or two students who get quite creative in their interpretation of these ideas. A student might say something like "You talking is impacting me and I'm not okay with that so you have to stop" or "I have to look at what you're wearing and it's impacting me and I don't like your outfit so you're not allowed to wear that anymore."

In moments like these, my classroom management strategy is as follows:

1. Acknowledge them (and maybe even praise them) for their creativity and understanding of the idea. When a student makes a statement like this, they are actually demonstrating that they understand the core concept of rights and, with that knowledge, are extrapolating on the concept. Students don't expect this kind of reaction to a "gotcha" comment like the ones above. This break in expectations will help the student be more open to what you say next.

2. At this point, I might use their own conceptualization to turn the statement around on them and, with a smile, remark that their question is having an impact on me, so I get to tell them to stop. I'll then remind the student that they are wise enough to understand the difference between jumping on someone's back without permission, telling someone that they can't talk, and requesting that someone speak more quietly because we're inside. I will then let the student know we're going to get into all of this in the coming lessons.

This is how I might handle situations like these. Use your own style here to help the student move away from the technical and into the deeper meaning. You can remind them that we all know that when we say "Give me a minute," we don't actually mean a minute. Similarly, when we say "If a decision impacts you and someone else, you both get a say," we don't actually mean that a person gets choice over *anything* they might be the slightest bit impacted by.

Step 5   Discussion

Prompt the class to reflect on the thoughts and feelings they're noticing in response to this conversation.

Students might share that certain people in their lives don't respect their bodily autonomy. If this becomes an abuse disclosure, follow your state and school guidelines for next steps. If the child is sharing the frustrating things their adults do that impose on their autonomy (bodily or otherwise), acknowledge this frustration. You might engage the class in thinking through why the adult has limited their autonomy in this way. You can also acknowledge that there are people who haven't learned about respecting people in this way or who think it's not important—and that this can be really hard. If you have the opportunity to engage with students' parents and caregivers about this, please do.

Give each student a copy of worksheet 1.2.1 to complete at home.

Supporting This Lesson in Your Classroom's Culture

- Connect decisions to reasons.
    - When a student wants to do something with their body that's not okay for them to do, consider the reason. If it's because it impacts other students, share that. If it's because it's a health and safety issue, share that. Help students understand that when there are rules, they're there for a reason. And if, as the teacher, you can't find a good reason, consider adjusting the rule.

- Connect decisions to rights.

  ○ When it seems like a student is physically bothering another student, your impulse might be to say something like "You can't do that" or "That's not nice." Instead, try asking the student, "Did you ask them if you could touch them like that?" This framing highlights that it's not about what the teacher wants; it's about what the other person involved wants. It reinforces the importance of asking questions of relevant parties, rather than following social scripts or just listening to those in power. Coach the student through the process of asking. If the friend says no, then problem solved. If the friend says they like it, but it's disruptive in this moment, you can encourage the two of them to continue during recess or another time.

- Highlight the role of choice and consequence.

  ○ If a student wants to color on their desk, you can say something like "Coloring happens on paper" or "Please don't color on the desk; it belongs to the school." You can also remind them of their ability to choose. I once had a 10-year-old student say to me, "You said I can't color on the desk." I corrected them, "You *can* color on the desk. That is a decision you can make, but there will be consequences to that decision. I am not going to physically grab the marker from your hand. If you choose to write on the desk, though, I won't have good reason to trust you to be responsible with markers in the future, so I probably just won't be willing to share them with you next time." When we remind students that they have the ability to choose, they have less reason to get into a power struggle with you (especially if they're regulated enough). If a student is going to do something imminently dangerous or wholly destructive, I will use my body to intervene. However, if I have the opportunity to help a student take responsibility for their own decisions, I will choose that option. When using this tool, be aware of the difference between natural consequences for their decisions and punishments for their noncompliance.

- Use phrases *other* than *bodily autonomy*.

  ○ If a student is challenging someone else's bodily autonomy, try saying, "It's their body, so they get to choose" or "They have to be part of the decision if it's about their body." While it's important that students understand what bodily autonomy is, it's more important that they connect with the value than the word. If you can use terminology and ideas that they're already familiar with and that they use in everyday speech, do so. A child who knows "Your body is yours" and treats classmates' bodies in alignment with this idea is what we're going for. Where we want to step in is when a child knows what bodily autonomy is but doesn't understand how to integrate that idea into practice.

Script 1.2.1

Teacher barges into student's house

STUDENT: What in the world are you doing here?

TEACHER: Don't worry about it. *snooping around as you please*

STUDENT: Can you at least take off your shoes? You're tracking mud everywhere.

TEACHER: Nah, I'm gonna wear my shoes. Besides, I'm the adult, you have to listen to me.

STUDENT: This is my house, though.

TEACHER: Well, you shouldn't have left the key in such an obvious hiding place.

Worksheet 1.2.1

Today, our class learned about bodily autonomy. *Bodily autonomy* means that your body is yours, so you get to make decisions about your body *and* you have the responsibility to make safe and kind decisions with your body. You get to choose what outfit you wear when you go to the park, *and* you need to watch where you're going when you're walking down a crowded street.

There are times when kids might not get to decide what their body does because it impacts others. For example, you need to use indoor voices when you're inside because loud voices might disturb others, and their bodies don't want that.

There are also times when bodily autonomy might be put on pause to keep your bodies healthy and safe. For example, adults tell kids that they need to wear seat belts because it's an adult's job to keep kids safe.

In this activity, you'll explore who makes what choices in *your* home.

Directions:

- Using a **red** marker, circle the decisions you mostly get to make on your own.
- Using a **blue** marker, circle the decisions that your adults at home are a big part of.
- If you're not sure about a decision, leave it blank for now.

Whether you wear a seat belt	The outfit you wear to bed	Whether you play-wrestle your grown-up
Whether you go to the doctor	Whether you wear a jacket outside	What time you get into bed
Giving/getting hugs from family members	Whether you get a vaccination	How much you eat at dinner

Desires and Boundaries

Learning Objectives:

By the end of this lesson, students will be able to:

1. Define what desires and boundaries are.

2. Identify some of their own desires and boundaries.

3. Demonstrate awareness of the individuality and flexibility of desires and boundaries.

4. Describe why it's important to respect boundaries.

Materials:

- Worksheet 1.3.1
- Whiteboard
- Whiteboard markers

Before You Start:

- Read through the lesson plan.
- Print worksheet 1.3.1 (one per student).

Time:
35 minutes

Step 1   Introduce the Topic

Guide the class in taking two deep breaths.

"So far, we've spoken about the practice of consent as doing more than just making sure that you have permission. We've discussed that it involves putting in the effort to consider yourself and the other person when making decisions that impact both of you—giving space for what you want, what you're okay with, and what you're not okay with, and giving space for what the other person wants, what they're okay with, and what they're not okay with."

"Today we're going to go deeper into what it means to consider yourself and the other person. We're going to start by simplifying the definition of *practicing consent*."

Write the following on the board: "The practice of consent is the practice of navigating your desires and boundaries *and* the other person's desires and boundaries."

Then say, "This is going to be our simpler definition of *practicing consent.*

"Today we're going to talk about desires and boundaries. In our next lesson, we're going to talk about what it means to 'navigate' or 'take care of.' When we practice consent, we care for our desires and boundaries and another person's desires and boundaries."

Step 2   Activity

Ask the class, "What is a desire?"

After students answer, say, "A desire is a feeling of wanting to have or do something. Sometimes we're aware of our desires, like you might be aware that you want ice cream. Sometimes, however, we're unaware of our desires. Like, you might want to sleep but be so cranky that you don't realize it. Sometimes you might want something to happen, but you don't want to do the work it takes to get there. Like, you might want your homework to be done but not want to do your homework. Throughout our lessons, we'll be using the words *desire* and *want* to mean the same thing."

In the following game, students will get a sense of the different desires of the people around them. Introduce the activity and its rules to your students.

Here is how the game works: Stand in a circle with your students. You will make a statement about something you want to do. All students who share that same desire will come into the center of the circle. All students who don't share that desire will stay where they are. Then everyone returns to their place in the circle. After you've modeled a couple of statements, you can allow students to share some too. If you choose to do this, put ground rules on the kinds of statements they can share. The following are some example statements and example ground rules for when students share their statements.

EXAMPLE STATEMENTS:

- "I want to play tag at recess."
- "I want to drink a cold glass of lemonade right now."
- "I want to eat a Greek salad for dinner tonight."
- "I want to wake up early tomorrow."
- "I want to get a pet dog."
- "I want to take a nap."

EXAMPLE GROUND RULES TO CONSIDER:

- Statements won't include specific people's names or refer to a specific person.

- Statements won't include violent behaviors or words.

After you've finished the activity, invite students back to their seats for a discussion.

DISCUSSION QUESTIONS:

- What did you notice about people's desires? Did we all have the same wants?

  - *Talking points:* Highlight how different people have different wants/desires. These are all valid. We are all unique and dynamic individuals. It's easy to assume that others feel the way you feel or want what you want, but that's often not the reality.

- If I said that I want tacos for dinner, is it okay for me to later share that I actually want lasagna for dinner? Why or why not?

  - *Talking points:* It's totally okay! Our desires will change. It's more than okay to notice a new desire. We have to also recognize that we don't always get what we desire. If a friend and I decide we're going to make tacos for dinner, I might recognize a new desire for lasagna, but that doesn't mean that now the plan switches to lasagna, because my friend might not want lasagna. I might decide to tell my friend about my new desire to see what works for them, or I might not. Part of practicing consent is understanding what our desires are and deciding how to include them in our decisions and interactions.

- Is it possible to know what someone wants without talking to them or communicating with them in some way?

  - *Talking points:* We might be able to *guess* what a person wants, based on what we know about them and their general likes, and there are times when we will be right. But our wants can change from day to day and moment to moment, so it's important to talk to the person about their specific wants in that moment. For example, I love burgers. But if you give me a burger after I've just had a whole lot of pizza, you wouldn't be giving me what I want.

"Now that we have a general understanding of what a desire is, let's talk about boundaries."

Ask students if they know what a boundary is. After hearing their responses, say, "A boundary separates two things from each other, like how the sidewalk separates your front yard, where it's safe to play, from the street, where it's not safe to play.

"We're going to be using *boundary* to describe the difference between what is okay and what isn't okay, as well as the difference between what is comfortable enough and what is too uncomfortable. You can also think of a boundary as a limit, or a point at which something is no longer comfortable enough or no longer okay, like how the edge of your front yard is the limit of where it's safe to play. Throughout our lessons, we'll be using the words *boundary* and *limit* to mean the same thing.

"Here are some ways you might hear the word *boundary* in a sentence." Read the following examples:

- "'I have a conversation boundary that I do not talk about my health needs with strangers.'—This means that I am not okay with talking about my health needs (the medications I take or the doctors I see) with strangers.

- "'Please don't ignore my body boundaries. I asked you not to touch my hair.'— This is how someone might let a friend know that they're not allowed to touch the asker's hair because that's beyond what the asker is okay with.

- "'What are your boundaries when it comes to me posting pictures of you on social media?'—This question tells your friend that you care about what they are and are not comfortable with when it comes to sharing their image online. Maybe they're comfortable with you sharing their image on a private account or only sharing their picture if they approve it first. Maybe they're not comfortable having their image shared by others at all.

"Think back to our conversation last time about who gets to make decisions. In these examples, the speaker recognizes their right to make a decision about their health privacy, their right to make a decision about their body (specifically their hair), and other people's right to make decisions about *their* image and how it's shared.

"Telling other people our boundaries helps us protect our right to make decisions about the things that are ours (our bodies, our stuff, our information, our time). Asking about and respecting friends' boundaries helps us protect their right to make decisions about the things that are theirs (their bodies, their stuff, their information, their time)."

Ask the class if they have any boundaries or limits around how pictures of them are shared online or who's allowed to touch their face or hair.

Then continue, "Boundaries can be communicated verbally, like 'I don't want a hug' or 'I'm stuffed; no more cake for me!' Boundaries can also be communicated visually, like with a poster that says 'Keep out!' or a shake of the head that means no.

"Just like desires, boundaries are clearly communicated sometimes, but not always. What if there is no sign? What if a friend hasn't said anything to you about what they are and are not okay with? We can often find ourselves in these situations. Your friend doesn't come over for a playdate with a list of likes and dislikes for the day. You don't walk into your classroom and start reciting for your classmates how you are and are not okay being touched. It would be impossible to keep up with! Remember that our minds can change from moment to moment and from person to person.

"You probably don't want to spend all day, every day, listing your boundaries and desires. You probably also don't want to be in situations where your friend is totally unaware of what you want and what you're okay with, or situations where you're totally unaware of what your friend wants or is okay with. Thankfully, these aren't the only options. We're going to talk a lot about boundaries throughout these lessons. Today, we're going to start by looking at some of our general boundaries."

Step 4 Activity

"Boundaries are similar to desires in that they communicate what you want or don't want. The first thing to know about boundaries is that you have the right to your boundaries and others have a right to theirs. The next three things to know are:

1. We all have different boundaries.

2. We all have different boundaries with different people.

3. Boundaries can change."

Introduce worksheet 1.3.1 to the class and review the instructions. Give students about six minutes to complete the worksheet. Once students have completed the worksheet, you can ask them if they're willing to share some of their responses. Be sure to remind students not to name names.

"The phrase *They crossed my boundary* means that someone did something that was outside of your comfort zone, outside of what you're okay with. For example, I might say that Shayla crossed Will's boundary when she jumped on his bed without asking."

Ask the class why it's important to do our best not to cross other people's boundaries. Focus the conversation on how crossing someone's boundary can cause hurt bodies and hurt feelings. Remind students about bodily autonomy and who gets to choose. If a decision impacts another person's body, that person needs to be included in the decision-making.

Explain, "We can't just do whatever we want. We need permission if we want to borrow a friend's toy, jump on a friend's bed, or touch a friend's body."

Supporting This Lesson in Your Classroom's Culture

- Acknowledge students' desires.

  ○ When a student shares a desire, take a moment to acknowledge the desire before moving on. If they say, "I want pizza for lunch," try saying, "Oh, pizza sounds good, what kind of pizza would you want?" or "You're noticing you want pizza. I'm noticing that sounds good to me too." When we engage students in this way, we help them build their skills in noticing their desires and reinforce the joy we can experience when we notice and share desires.

  ○ Try reacting this way to their disappointment about *unfulfilled* desires too. When a student is disappointed that they didn't get what they want (e.g., a student says, "But I wanted pizza" after seeing their parent packed a bagel for lunch), we don't need to fix their frustration or try to change their desires to match the situation ("Oh, I'm sure the bagel will hit the spot!"). Instead, we can empathize and reflect the situation back to them ("You noticed you wanted pizza, but you have a bagel in your lunchbox."). This approach subtly reinforces the value of noticing desires, reminds students that it's okay to have desires that go unfulfilled, and tells students that they can handle the disappointment of not getting what they want.

- Be proactive about sharing your personal boundaries and the boundaries of the classroom.

  ○ If a student isn't aware of a boundary, we can't necessarily expect them to respect the boundary. Sometimes we don't recognize that we have a boundary or that we need to communicate a boundary until it gets crossed. When this happens, acknowledge that this is something that the student didn't know before, but now that they know about it, they are expected to respect it.

- Acknowledge students' boundaries.

  - When a student shares a boundary, we again want to engage them in what they notice in themselves. Take a moment to acknowledge the boundary before moving on to problem-solving. You can say "Thank you for sharing that limit with me" or "You're telling me you're not comfortable with that. I really appreciate you letting me know." We don't want to shut down boundaries; we want to embrace them.

- Consider your options when a student is having a hard time accepting or understanding a boundary.

  - You can:

    - Empathize with them about how it can be difficult and disappointing to hear a new boundary.

    - Connect it to a reason they can understand.

    - Invite them into something that they can do (e.g., if the boundary is no spitting on friends in class, invite them to use outdoor recess as a chance to see how far onto the grass they can spit. Yes, this is a real idea.).

  - Reinforce that boundaries don't take away the fun; they help us have fun safely.

  - Some students will have an especially hard time when boundaries change or when different boundaries apply to different people. In addition to empathizing with them, reference their completed worksheet 1.3.1 to remind them that this is the way boundaries work for everyone.

Worksheet 1.3.1

We all have boundaries. Time to get familiar with yours!

Directions: Think about your boundaries. First, come up with three boundaries you have that others don't have (or boundaries that others have but you don't have). Next, come up with three boundaries that apply to some people in your life but not to other people. Last, come up with three boundaries in your life that have changed over time (or that might change in the future).

Hint: If you're having a hard time thinking about boundaries, think about the rules you have for yourself around your body, your room, your toys, your meals, or your screen time. You can also think about what you are and are not willing to do with friends and family.

We all have different boundaries.

In each box, name a boundary you have that is different from someone else's boundary.

- **Example:** *I won't eat cheesecake, but my best friend loves it.*

Your Boundaries:

1.

2.

3.

We have different boundaries with different people.

In each box, name a boundary you have with one person that is different from your boundary with someone else.

- **Example:** *I love goodnight hugs from my dad, but I'm not okay with getting them from my babysitter.*

Your Boundaries:

1.

2.

3.

Boundaries can change.

In each box, name a boundary you have now that is different from what your boundary used to be.

- **Example:** *I didn't always like having friends in my room, but now I'm okay with it.*

Your Boundaries:

1.

2.

3.

Navigating Consent

Learning Objectives:

By the end of this lesson students will be able to:

1. Describe what it means to navigate two people's boundaries and desires.

2. Identify how a person can better care for their own desires and boundaries and care for others' desires and boundaries.

3. Describe the importance of caring for oneself and for someone else.

Materials:

- Whiteboard
- Whiteboard markers

Before You Start:

- Read through the lesson plan.
- Review the book *The Giving Tree*, by Shel Silverstein.

Time:
25 minutes

Step 1   Introduce the Topic

Write the following on the board: "The practice of consent is the practice of navigating your desires and boundaries *and* the other person's desires and boundaries."

Guide the class in taking two deep breaths.

"In our lessons so far, we've talked about who gets to make certain decisions (and why) and we've talked about what desires and boundaries are. Today we're going to explore what it means to *navigate* boundaries and desires so we can create relationships that feel good and where both people feel respected."

Ask the class, "What does *navigate* mean?"

After students answer, say, "*To navigate* means to steer, to travel, or to find your way through something. This word comes from the Latin word for *ship*. That's why we use this word when talking about sailors finding their way across oceans and seas. They navigate their ship.

"When we practice consent, we aren't traveling across any oceans or seas. In this context, *to navigate* means 'to find your way through an interaction' with care and respect for yourself and others. Let's explore how using the word *navigation* in our definition of practicing consent can help us better understand what it means to practice consent."

Step 2   Discussion

Introduce the following metaphor: "If you're sailing a ship across an ocean, you need to rely on more than just a map or a set of directions. You need to consider a number of other factors. What is your ideal route? What is your plan B and your plan C in case plan A falls through? What kind of boat is it? Do you have experience steering this kind of boat? What is the weather supposed to be like? What is your plan if the weather changes? What is the purpose of this journey? Is this a voyage you've been on before? What skills do you have? Who's on the ship with you? Who are the crew? What skills do they have?"

Ask students what else a person might need to navigate a ship across the ocean.

After students answer, say, "When it comes to navigating across the sea, there's no one set of directions or instructions that we can always follow. The path to get safely to shore today won't necessarily be the path for getting safely to shore tomorrow. The way you navigate this ocean, in this weather, might not be the same way you need to navigate that ocean, in that weather. Sometimes there are many routes you can take to reach your destination safely. There are also certain routes that will put you and your crew at risk. If you take those routes, you might not even get to your destination at all. And sometimes you will veer off course, but as long as you don't veer too far, you can get back on track and safely get yourself and your crew where you want to be.

"When it comes to navigating ships, there's no step-by-step guide that works in every situation. There's not even a set of directions that we can rely on in a single scenario. The weather might change, a crew member might get sick, or a cloudy night might get in the way of reading the stars. When someone navigates, they need to be ready to change their approach based on what's happening. I'm not going to feel safe on a sea voyage where the captain only knows how to follow one set of directions. I'm going to feel safe on a voyage where the captain has the skills to navigate and shift plans as circumstances change.

"Our relationships aren't so different from sailing ships. When it comes to creating and maintaining healthy, safe, and fun relationships, there's no one set of directions or instructions that we can always follow. When someone is navigating a ship across the ocean, they are paying attention to the waves, the weather, the crew, the boat, and so on, and using their knowledge and skills to make safe and smart decisions that lead them to shore.

"When you are practicing consent, you are paying attention to your desires and boundaries *and* the other person's desires and boundaries. You are using your knowledge and skills to make caring and respectful decisions that will allow you to have healthy, safe, and fun relationships and interactions. This what it means to *navigate* in the practice of consent."

Step 3   Activity

"We talked about what a person needs to consider while navigating a ship across the sea. Now we're going to explore what a person needs to consider while navigating an interaction with a friend."

Ask a student to recap the story of *The Giving Tree*. Specifically, have them recall what might have been going on in the boy's mind and in the tree's mind throughout their interactions. Remind them of your discussion in lesson 1.1.

Once students' memories are jogged, ask, "What did the boy do that supported a strong consent practice? What did the boy pay attention to, consider, say to the tree, or ask the tree when making some of his decisions?"

As students respond, generate a list on the board based on their answers. Leave room for a second column.

After that list feels complete, ask about the tree: "What did the tree do that supported a strong consent practice? What did the tree pay attention to, consider, say to the boy, or ask the boy when making some of her decisions?"

At the end, your lists might look something like:

WHAT DID THE BOY DO WELL?

- Was clear about his desires
- Seemed to express his appreciation for the tree by giving hugs and carving initials
- Was clear about not being interested in climbing or swinging when he was older

WHAT DID THE TREE DO WELL?

- Gave space for the boy's desires
- Offered the things she had available to offer

Then say, "Now that we've talked about what both characters did well, let's explore how they can improve on their consent practice (on their ability to care for and respect both of their desires and boundaries) moving forward."

Ask, "What do you think the boy in the story can do differently next time to better practice consent? What can the boy pay attention to, consider, say to the tree, or ask the tree when making some of his decisions?"

As students respond, generate a list on the board based on their answers. Leave room for a second column.

After that list feels complete, ask about the tree: "What do you think the tree in the story can do differently next time to better practice consent? What can the tree pay attention to, consider, say to the boy, or ask the boy when making some of her decisions?" (Module 4 dives deeply into why saying no is hard, especially when there is a skewed power dynamic. We need to hold space for why it might be hard for the tree to say no and hold space for what skills she can work on for the future.)

At the end, your lists might look something like:

WHAT CAN THE BOY DO NEXT TIME?

- Ask the tree how she would like to play

- Ask the tree what she wants

- Talk to the tree about what's going on in her life

- Double-check to see if the tree is really okay with giving what she is giving

- Ask if there are any strings attached to her gifts

- Start a conversation about how often they plan to see each other

- Pay attention to her body language or tone of voice

- Recognize that he is only focused on his wants

- Consider that he can move around but she can't and how that plays a role in their relationship

- Apologize for taking all of her resources

WHAT CAN THE TREE DO NEXT TIME?

- Share how she's feeling

- Share her wants

- Tell the boy that she wants to see him more often

- Start a conversation about how often they plan to see each other

- Ask the boy what he's tried to do to make money before giving him apples

- Tell the boy that she is no longer willing to help him by giving him all of her resources

- Share her boundaries

- Recognize that she is only focused on his wants

- Take responsibility for not being clear about her wants

DISCUSSION QUESTIONS:

- Is it fair to say that it's the tree's responsibility to look after her own wants and limits (and that it's not the boy's responsibility)? Is it also fair to say that it's the boy's responsibility to "only" look after his own wants and limits? (Why does he have to focus on the tree?)

  - *Talking points:* There is something to be said for us being responsible for ourselves. We absolutely want to do our best to tend to our own wants and limits. But it doesn't have to be either/or. We can tend to our own wants and limits *and* tend to others' wants and limits. Friendships are so wonderful because they are support systems. If you're having a hard time expressing your wants, a friend can help you out. If a friend is having a hard time sharing their limits, you can help them out. If we only focused on ourselves, we'd have a very selfish and divided world.

- Looking at these lists, do you think the tree and the boy have to do *all* of these things to practice consent well?

  - *Talking points:* No, but there's a lot they could have done. Even doing one of these things could have totally changed the trajectory of their relationship. If the boy had taken a moment to check in on what the tree wanted, or if the tree had taken a moment to share her expectations, a totally different story could have unfolded.

  - Playwright Topher Payne wrote an alternate ending to *The Giving Tree* that illustrates exactly this. It can be found at https://www.topherpayne.com/giving-tree. It's a wonderful supplement to this lesson.

Conclude this lesson by saying, "You now have a better understanding of what it means to practice consent. As we move through the coming lessons, we're going to talk about and practice specific skills that will help us do better in our practice of consent so that we can be in relationships where we are acting with more awareness, care, and respect and being treated with more awareness, care, and respect."

Supporting This Lesson in Your Classroom's Culture

- Acknowledge that practicing consent isn't simple.

  - If practicing consent were simple, the rates of sexual assault wouldn't be what they are and this book wouldn't exist. While the practice of consent can and should be simplified to help students learn in a developmentally appropriate and scaffolded way, the practice of consent isn't simple. There is vulnerability in asking, saying no, checking in, and being accountable. Navigating social pressures and norms alongside complicated beliefs about ourselves and potentially difficult emotions is no easy task. Even when we do find a way to work with the vulnerability of noticing and communicating honestly about our desires and boundaries *and* the other person's desires and boundaries, we can't read minds. None of us can know with certainty why someone is saying yes to an interaction or how they feel about the various lines of power at play.

  - Consent is a dynamic and ongoing practice. When you notice a student struggling to use a certain consent skill, try helping them understand what's getting in the way. It can be tempting to respond to a skill deficit by saying something like "It's important to do this" or "Part of being a good friend is doing XYZ." Try to also include questions like "What about this is hard right now?" or "What's getting in the way of you doing XYZ?" or "What would make doing XYZ easier?" Follow with "And why do you think that is?" Questions such as these will help students develop greater self-awareness and allow them to come up with their own solutions in the future and use skills in navigating their boundaries and desires alongside others' boundaries and desires.

MODULE 2

I Ask for What I Want

Noticing My Wants

Time:
15 minutes

Learning Objectives:

By the end of this lesson, students will be able to:

1. Recognize that their bodies provide them information on how they feel.

2. Describe how observing their bodies can help them make decisions.

Materials:

- Whiteboard
- Whiteboard markers

Before You Start:

- Read through the lesson plan.

Step 1   Introduce the Topic

Guide the class in taking two deep breaths.

"Over the next few lessons, we're going to be focusing on asking—specifically on asking for what we want. But before we get to how to ask for what we want, we need to make sure we all know how to figure out what we want. After all, before you ask your adult to make you something for dinner, you need to know what you want for dinner."

Ask each student to share what food they want for dinner tonight.

Then discuss:

1. Whether it was easy or hard for them to figure out what they want for dinner.

2. How they figured out what they wanted for dinner. Prompt students to consider if they noticed any shifts in their bodies as they were making their choice or as they landed on their answer.

"Sometimes it's easy to know what you want, and sometimes it's harder. We're going to learn a way to help you figure out what you want when you're not sure."

"Close your eyes. Take a big breath in and out. I'm going to read a list of words. As I do so, I want you to pay attention to your body."

Read the following list. Pause between each word. When you're finished reading the list, invite students to gently open their eyes.

WORD LIST:

- Pizza
- Puppies
- Spiders
- Coffee

- Cats
- Rotten eggs
- Chocolate
- Ice cream

- Homework
- The beach
- Hiking
- Roller coasters

DISCUSSION QUESTIONS:

- How did that feel? What did you notice?

  - *Talking points:* There's no right answer. Students might share what they noticed about their bodies during the activity or what they notice about their bodies now.

- Which words left the biggest impression?

  - *Talking points:* There's no right answer. As students share, prompt them to consider what kind of impression the word (or words) left.

- Were there any words that made you feel especially good? What did you notice in your body when you heard those words?

  - *Talking points:* People often notice a slight smile on their face with either a very relaxed face or very excited face (where their eyebrows are raised).

"Slowing down and paying attention to our bodies allow us to gather information about how we feel and what sounds good in a given moment. Once we have that information, we're more prepared to ask for what we want and more likely to make decisions that we feel good about.

"Thinking back to the question of what you want for dinner tonight, you can use this same strategy. If you're having a hard time figuring out what you want, you can ask your adult to list some options. Take a deep breath and maybe even close your eyes and consider what your body reacts to with excitement or joy. Then, you can request that option. You can do the same when a friend asks you what you want to do when they're at your house or what they want to play during recess. If someone asks you a yes-or-no question, you can also use this strategy. Pay attention to how your body reacts when they ask, 'Would you like to play a game of tag?' or 'Would you like to do a puzzle with me?'"

Step 3   Discussion

Share the following scenario with your students: "Imagine that you're relaxing on the couch watching TV when, all of a sudden, you realize you'd really like some lemonade. A cold glass of lemonade sounds so good to you right now. Just the thought of it is bringing a smile to your face and making your mouth water. The desire is real. There's some lemonade in the basement pantry, but it feels so far away and you're so comfy. In our last lesson, we talked about the importance of respecting and caring for our desires. Does that mean you're being disrespectful to and uncaring toward yourself if you decide not to get up and get yourself the lemonade?"

After students respond, say, "Being respectful and caring about your desires means you take the time to pay attention to your desires and to recognize that your desires are important. You don't have to follow through on every desire you have. You have a choice, which means you get to choose what desires to follow through on. You get to decide when you want to put in the effort to go downstairs and get the lemonade and when you want to stay right where you are. It would be uncaring to yourself if you tried to convince yourself that you didn't have any desires or that your desires didn't matter. You get to choose what you do with the wants you have."

Supporting This Lesson in Your Classroom's Culture

Model It

- Vocalize what you notice about your body when making decisions.

    ○ If a student asks if you will play with them, you can respond with "Hm, I'm noticing my body is feeling heavy and tired. I don't have the capacity to play today. Can we play tomorrow if I'm feeling more energetic?" or "That question lit me up. I noticed the smile on my face as soon as you asked. I'd love to play." Speaking to how you pay attention to your body and use that information in your decision-making process will show them how they can do the same.

Coach It

- Cue your students to pause and pay attention to their bodies before responding.

  - As teachers, we're often in a rush, trying to fit everything we need to get done into the limited time we have. We might tell kids, "Decide already" or "Stop changing your mind." While a prompt to focus can be helpful for the student (and for the class), sometimes the situation calls for a moment of slowness rather than a push for speed.

  - When a student is struggling to make a decision, consider inviting them to pause, take a deep breath, and listen to what their body is saying. A deep breath helps the body and mind slow down. When we feel rushed by others (or by our own internal monologues), being still enough to pay attention to the body becomes a challenge. A reminder that it's okay to pause can go a long way. Use this reminder for yourself and for your students.

- Remind students that they don't have to follow their desires.

  - If a student tells you that they want to invite a friend to their sleepover but they're nervous that the friend will say no, your job is to help them decide what they want to do with that desire. It could be they want encouragement in turning that desire into a request (to be discussed in lesson 2.2), or they might just want to sit there noticing their desire and not take any action yet. In a moment like this, if the student decides that they don't want encouragement or support in taking action, you can remind them that their choice is theirs to make and that it's great that they noticed their want. A lot of people struggle to notice their desires or just ignore them. If we were responsible for fulfilling *all* desires, they would become restrictive burdens. Just like it's okay for you to notice you want to go on an expensive vacation but not buy the ticket, it's okay for your student to notice they have a want and not fulfill it.

Requests

Learning Objectives:

By the end of this lesson students will be able to:

1. Describe what a request is.

2. Describe the barriers to making requests.

3. Reflect on why we need to get comfortable making requests and the importance of creating friendships where both people have the opportunity to ask for what they want.

4. Use practical experience to improve their request practices.

Materials:

• Whiteboard

• Whiteboard markers

Before You Start:

• Read through the lesson plan.

• Decide how you will pair up students in step 4.

Step 1   Demo

Ask for a student to volunteer to help you with a short and silly demonstration. If no students are willing, ask another teacher to play the student role.

With the student volunteer at the front of the class, read the following list of requests. This works best when the student starts to fulfill the request, but you make another request before they have time to actually complete it. The more movement there is (from you and from them), the more engaging this demonstration will be.

REQUESTS:

• "May I have your pencil?"

• "Will you write your name on the board?"

• "Can you please turn the lights off?"

- "Please turn them back on."

- "Will you allow me to sit in your chair?"

- "Please give me your pen."

- "Would you tell me your favorite color?"

- "Will you please return to your seat?"

Invite the class to give a round of applause and thank the student for participating.

Guide the class in taking two deep breaths.

DEBRIEF:

Ask students to describe what just happened. The goal is for students to recognize that *you* were making requests.

Often, students will point out that the volunteer student was doing things that the teacher asked them to do. If this is the case in your classroom, point out that while this is mostly true, there's an exception. The question "Will you allow me to sit in your chair?" reveals that it's about more than just who the doer is. It's not about who is *doing* the action (that is, the volunteer student) but about *who the action was for* (the teacher). Said another way, it was about the teacher's wants/desires.*

OPTIONAL DISCUSSION QUESTIONS:

- "When I was making requests, I was quickly asking our student volunteer to do things I wanted them to do. But I was making requests really quickly. How much do you think my requests were about what I really want and how much were they about getting my way?"

- "Have you ever made requests just to get your way?" Here you can share a story about a time you purposely disagreed with your sibling, friend, or parent just to get your way (e.g., "My brother requested to get pizza for dinner, but I was annoyed at him that day, so I intentionally requested we get burgers instead even though I love pizza.") Make space for a discussion about why we do this, whether this is kind, and what we can do instead.

---

* For expanded information on the relationship between who is doing and who something is for, see *The Art of Receiving and Giving: The Wheel of Consent* (Martin & Dalzen, 2021).

"In our last lesson, we learned about how our bodies can give us information about what we want and what we don't want. Once you know what you want, you can take steps to possibly getting what you want. By a show of hands, who likes getting what they want?

"Sometimes we go about getting what we want by just doing. If I'm at home sitting on the couch and I want to go to the bathroom, I just get up and do it. If I'm coloring as part of free play and I want to draw a dog, I can just do it.

"But we can't *always* do things we want to do just because we want to do them. I might want to use a friend's markers. But unless I've already talked with my friend about using their markers, it's not okay for me to just get up and take them. I might want to play tag with a sibling, but I can't just make that decision on my own. I might want to lie down in the car while my dad is driving, but I can't just decide to do that because I want to."

Ask the class to name reasons why it might not be okay to do something just because you want to do it. Prompt students to consider the scenarios you just described. Simplify their answers and write them on the board.

The list might include answers like:

- Because of safety

- Because it's not healthy

- Because it impacts other people

- Because you need to ask first

- Because it's not kind

- Because an adult said it's not okay (You can write this on the board if a student shares this; we'll come back to this later.)

"This is a great list. Today we're going to focus on what you can do when you notice you want something, but because it impacts someone else or it involves someone else, you need to ask first or make a request. 'Making a request' is just another way of saying 'asking for what you want.'"

Use hand-raising to take a class poll. Ask students to indicate whether they think making requests is (a) always easy, (b) always hard, or (c) sometimes easy and sometimes hard. Invite some students to share their reasoning.

As they share, create two lists on the board titled "Why Is Making Requests Hard?" and "What Makes Making Requests Easier?" and organize their reasons on the respective lists.

Your lists might look something like:

WHY IS MAKING REQUESTS HARD?

- They might say no.

- They'll think you're needy.

- You like being a giver, not a taker.

- It's hard to ask people you don't know well.

- It might be embarrassing.

- You might get an answer you don't like.

WHAT MAKES MAKING REQUESTS EASIER?

- Remembering that it's okay if they say no

- Feeling confident

- Feeling like they won't make fun of you

- When you're making a request of somebody who you're close to

- When you're making requests of a younger sibling
  (when you have more authority)

Ask students what resonates. Acknowledge that sometimes making a request or asking for what you want can be challenging. Affirm that, together, you're going to learn ways to overcome some of those challenges because the more we can get better at asking for what we want, the more likely we are to get the things we want and the more honest we can be in our friendships!

Step 3   Discussion

"Asking for what we want is great because it helps us get what we want, but it's also important because when we have wants and don't share those wants openly and honestly, they can sometimes show themselves in sneaky ways." This is a concept known as "desire smuggling" (Baczynski & Scott, 2022).

"What do people do when they have a desire, but making a request feels too challenging?"

You can give examples to help clarify what you're asking (e.g., "What might you do if you want someone to share their snack but are too nervous to ask?").

Invite students to share their answers. Answers might include:

- Just not get what you want

- Take it anyway

- Blame the other person for not mind-reading

- Get annoyed at the other person

- Ask the other person if they want something

- Ask for something you don't want

- Drop hints about what you want

- Try to make it seem like they want what you want

"Raise your hand if you've been told that asking for what you want is unkind or selfish."

After students raise their hands, ask, "Based on what we just discussed, do you think that's true? Is asking for what you want unkind or selfish? Think about what happens when we don't ask."

Invite students to respond. Acknowledge that (a) we can ask for something in an unkind way, or someone can ask for a lot without giving anything or much in return, and that (b) it wouldn't feel good to be in a relationship where, all or most of the time, only one friend is getting what they want. But recognizing what we want and asking for it (in a kind way) is actually a way of being honest, and when done with equal give-and-take, it helps *support* strong relationships.

Step 4   Practice

"With all of this in mind, we're going to practice asking for what we want, or making requests."

Explain the instructions for this practice.

PRACTICE INSTRUCTIONS:

1. Pair up students. Look at the *Guidelines for Pairing Up Students* at end of this lesson.

2. Each student will have a turn to practice asking for what they want (making requests).

3. Requests will begin with either "Will you . . . ?" or "May I . . .?"

   ○ Write these two phrases on the board.

   ○ Instruct students to take their time and think about what they really want. See the sample requests listed at the end of these steps.

4. Ask one student to start as the asker and the other as the listener.

5. The job of the listener is just to hear the request, not to answer.

6. The asker will make three requests. Then the students will switch roles. Once both students have made their three requests, have them raise their hands to indicate that they're done.

7. Invite a student to volunteer to help you model what this looks like. You'll be in the asker role with the student in the listening role.

SAMPLE REQUESTS:

- A gift or something someone might put on a holiday wish list

   ○ Example: Will you buy me a new LEGO set? Will you buy me a diamond necklace? Will you bring me a glass of fruit punch?

- A turn with something they own

   ○ Example: May I borrow your video game console? May I take home your dog for the night?

- An experience together

   ○ Example: Will you come with me to the amusement park? Will you play with me at recess?

DISCUSSION QUESTIONS:

- What did you notice while doing that?

- How did it feel to make requests?

- What was the experience of coming up with requests like?

- What was the experience of actually making the requests like?

- Were you thinking about how the listener would react?

Wrap up the lesson by highlighting the following:

- While we *can* make requests in an unkind way, asking for what we want isn't rude or selfish.

- In a strong friendship, both people have a chance to request what they want (and both people feel safe to say no—to be discussed later).

- We talked about what can make asking harder, and we're going to explore what we can do in those moments next time.

Supporting This Lesson in Your Classroom's Culture

Model It

- Make sure *your* requests are being balanced with offers.

  - As a teacher, you're responsible for guiding the class. You're in charge of making sure that everything runs smoothly and that work gets done. From "Will someone come up to the board to answer this?" to "Please stop coloring on the desk," you're making requests throughout the day. To help strengthen your relationship with students and create mutuality, find time to make offers. Find out what students want to do and offer them the opportunity to do those things they want. As the person in the room with power (we'll talk more about that later), you have the ability to *empower* your students by showing them that their desires matter too.

Coach It

- Celebrate desires and support students in asking for what they want.

  - When opportunities arise, coach students to make requests. Although there may be times when it's easier and more appropriate to make a request on behalf of a student (e.g., "Xander, will you let Smadar borrow a pencil?"), support students in making a request themselves when you can. Support might look like helping them practice with you beforehand, coming up with the right words, empathizing with them around why they want you to ask for them, or problem-solving around what they will do if they hear a no.

  - It's also okay to have a desire and not want to do anything about it. There's an important difference between "I want you to ask instead of me" and "I don't want anyone to ask."

- Make sure students are balancing their requests with offers.

  - Tune into your students' interactions during free play, recess, and group projects. Is there one student making a lot of requests and only focusing on what they want? Are students making space for others' wants too? It's okay if one student is leading play, but that leader can make both requests and offers. Offers sound like "What game would you like to play next?" or "Would you like a turn on this?"

  - It's more important to address and intervene if you notice this as a specific student's pattern across situations or interactions. Work with them to navigate their desires along with the desires of others.

Guidelines for Pairing Up Students

Pairing up students is often a challenge. When you prioritize choice and let students pick their partners, some students will feel left out, some students will be caught in analysis paralysis (unable to decide whom to partner with), and some students will end up in partnerships in which they're likely to be distracted. At the same time, when you pick the partnerships yourself, students might end up in situations where they don't feel comfortable. In the context of learning about consent, this is especially challenging to justify.

There is no right answer here. My recommendation is to be responsive to the class at hand. Here are suggestions for creating partnerships that uphold the idea that students get choice in decisions that impact them:

1. Give students some choice:

   - Get two colors of sticky notes. Write each student's name on a note and stick them on a wall. Have each student find their name and then find a partner whose name is written on a different color note.

   - Have students partner with anyone in their row of desks, in their desk pod, at the desk pod across from them, in the row behind them, or as works best for your classroom.

2. Ask students if they want partners to be picked randomly by an online generator.

   - There are online tools that you can use to create random pairs. Sometimes students will feel better about choices that are left totally to chance rather than choices that are made intentionally by others. If students choose this option, they are getting some choice already.

Whichever option you choose, you can empathize with students' frustrations and give space for collaboration. It's frustrating when we don't get total choice, so it makes sense for students to be frustrated. But there are reasons that you're making these choices. Share that you're open to other suggestions and collaboration. You might not have time to hear their suggestion in the moment, but you can set aside time to talk to them later and genuinely consider their idea.

Being a Better Asker

Learning Objectives:

By the end of this lesson, students will be able to:

1. Demonstrate how to make requests in a way that acknowledges others' interests.

2. Demonstrate how to effectively turn commands and assumptions into questions.

3. Describe how to make it easier for others to give their honest answers.

Time:
25 minutes

Materials:

- Worksheet 2.3.1
- Handout 2.3.1
- Flip chart paper
- Flip chart markers
- Whiteboard
- Whiteboard markers

Before You Start:

- Read through the lesson plan.
- Print worksheet 2.3.1 (one per student).
- Print handout 2.3.1 (one per student).

Step 1   Introduce the Topic

Guide the class in taking two deep breaths.

"In our last lesson, we talked about how making requests, or asking for what we want, *and* making room for others to make requests helps support healthy relationships.

"Today we're going to focus on *how* to make requests or invite friends to do something with you in a way that will feel good for you and for them."

Introduce the model *Express, Invite, Offer* (Harrison, 2020).

"Express, Invite, Offer is a simple way to ask someone if they would like to do something with you."

Write the following on the board:

1. **Express** interest.

2. **Invite** them to participate.

3. **Offer** an alternative.

Then give an example:

1. "**I want to** play tag."

2. "**Are you in?**"

3. "**Or would you rather** play something else?"

Ask students to share why this is a great model for making a request. As they answer, reinforce that the Express, Invite, Offer model allows room for both people's interests or wants.

Come up with your own examples together and write them on the board using the same format as the following table.

Review the first example and then, as a class, come up with two more examples of requests that (1) express interest, (2) invite a person to participate, and (3) offer an alternative.

Express	Invite	Offer
I'd love for you to make a braid in my hair.	Are you willing to do that? I can make a braid in yours in return.	Or we can just keep coloring instead.

Close out the activity by asking students if this is the only way to ask for something. Reinforce that, of course, it isn't. However, keeping this model in mind can help us make requests and offers that recognize both our perspective and the other person's. It can be in tool in speaking up for our desires while recognizing that the other person might have other interests too.

Step 3 Activity

"Another way a person might stumble when trying to make a request is by saying a statement instead of asking a question."

If it would support your students, review the difference between a statement and a question before continuing.

Introduce worksheet 2.3.1 to the class and review the instructions. Give students about five minutes to complete the worksheet. Once students have completed the worksheet, review the answers together. You can also do the whole worksheet together as a class.

Step 4 Discussion

"When you make a request, you open yourself up to hearing a no. That's one reason that making a request or inviting someone to share an experience with you can be nerve-racking or scary."

Ask the class how a person might feel after hearing a no. Affirm their answers.

"Even though hearing a no can be hard, part of being a good friend means giving space for our friends to be honest with themselves and with us, even when that means that we feel a sting of hard emotions as a result. We want to help our friends feel comfortable saying either yes or no." (In future lessons, you'll talk about why saying no or giving your true answer can be hard.)

Ask the class to share some things they can say or do while making requests to make it easier for friends to say no (or generally be honest in their answers). Hint: you've discussed some of them already.

Generate a list on a flip chart so you can hang it somewhere in your classroom.

Then give each student a copy of handout 2.3.1. Add any additional ideas to this list.

Refer to these tips when students are struggling with this skill.

Model It

- Ask curious questions.

  - Curious questions are most important when it comes to students' preferences, intentions, and interpretations. Review worksheet 2.3.1 and consider how you can change a statement into a curious question.

- Be a better asker with your students.

  - When making requests of your students (e.g., asking them to volunteer, go first, answer the question aloud), remind them that it's okay if they say no, give them opportunities to say yes to an alternative, and give them a chance to take time to decide so that they can make a choice that feels good.

Coach It

- Pay attention when you notice a student telling instead of asking.

  - Sometimes it's okay to ask instead of tell. It's most important to look out for students who are in conflict as a result of telling instead of asking a curious question or who have a habit of telling others how to play instead of asking them how they would like to engage in play. The phrase "Did you ask them?" is a great way to get things going. For example, "Did you ask them what role they wanted to play?" or "Did you ask them if you could borrow their pencil for the whole day?" If this is a pattern with a certain student, it might warrant further conversation about what you're noticing.

Worksheet 2.3.1

Telling isn't the same as asking.

Directions: Look at the statements below. Rewrite each statement as a curious question.

EXAMPLES:

Statement	Curious Question
You're going to have the best time at his party.	How do you feel about going to his party?
A playdate means hanging out and watching TV.	What do you want to do on this playdate?

Statement	Curious Question
You love when I jump on you!	
You should hug Ms. Johnson.	
Dogs are the best, so you have to pet her.	
Stop complaining. You love this recipe.	
You have to be the wizard today.	
You did that on purpose.	

Hint: Does your curious question end in a question mark?

Handout 2.3.1

If you want someone else to respond honestly to your request . . .

1. **Ask first.** Give them a chance to share their answer. If you want to give them a hug, it'll be easier for them to say no to the question "May I have a hug?" than to stop the action of you giving them a hug.

2. **Give them space to decide.** Giving someone time to decide allows them the opportunity to check in with how their body really feels. You can say something like "You don't need to decide now" or "Take a second to pause before you answer."

3. **Remind them that any answer they give is okay.** You can say something like "By the way, I'm cool with a yes or a no. I just want you to be honest" or "I'll be okay with any answer you give."

4. **Ask open-ended questions.** Instead of just asking questions that can be answered with a yes or no, you can ask questions that invite a friend to share more details. Instead of "Do you want to play outside?" you can say "I'd like to play outside. What would you like to do?"

5. **Offer an alternative.** When you make your request or put forth your invitation, give at least one other option. You can say something like "May I give you a hug goodbye? If you're not in the mood, maybe we could do a high five?" or "Would you like to hang out this weekend or next? If you're busy both weekends, that's okay too."

Getting Specific in Our Asks

Learning Objectives:

By the end of this lesson, students will be able to:

1. Demonstrate how to reduce assumptions by asking clarifying questions.

2. Describe how details can make all the difference when making decisions.

3. Recognize that we can't always know the reasons for someone's response.

Materials:

- Whiteboard
- Whiteboard markers

Before You Start:

- Read through the lesson plan.

Time: 25 minutes

Step 1   Introduce the Topic

Guide the class in taking two deep breaths.

"We've discussed how being curious about what you want *and* what others want is a key part of being able to practice consent. Today, we're going to talk about why our curiosity often needs to go beyond simply considering whether the other person says yes or no to your request."

Step 2   Activity

"We're going to start with a seated breath practice. Sit up tall in your seat. Roll your shoulders back. Imagine that a string extends from the top of your head all the way up to the ceiling, pulling your back straight and tall. Begin to breathe big, smooth breaths in through your nose and out through your nose.

"Close your eyes and imagine a beautiful field of flowers above you. Breathe in, reach up to the sky, and pluck a flower from the field. Imagine bringing it down toward your nose as you breathe out. When your imaginary flower is at your nose, take a deep breath in to smell its delicious scent, saying *ahhhhh* as you breathe out. Gently let your hands back down to your lap, and when you're ready, open your eyes."

DEBRIEF:

Ask the class how that felt. Then ask each student (or a couple of students) to describe the flower they imagined—how it looked and how it smelled.

When students are done sharing, bring their attention to the variation in their answers: "I want you to notice that when I said 'flower,' many of us imagined different kinds of flowers. In order for me to really know what you were imagining in your mind's eye, I had to ask for more detail, or more specific information. Even though I knew you were thinking about a flower, I didn't know anything about what kind of flower it was until we spoke more."

Connect the lesson to their everyday lives: "Think about going on a playdate. You might think a playdate means watching TV and playing video games, while your friend might think that a playdate means playing outside or in the park. No one is right or wrong. Rather, both friends need to speak to each other and ask questions to learn what the other person is thinking."

Step 3   Discussion

Explain that asking questions that draw out details is all about reducing, or making sure there are fewer, assumptions.

Ask the class what it means to assume. After you hear some responses, you can add, "*To assume* means you think you know something even though you haven't taken the time to investigate or ask questions."

You can ask a student to share an example of an assumption or share one yourself.

DISCUSSION QUESTIONS:

- How would you feel if I assumed what kind of ice cream you wanted for your birthday instead of asking you? How would you feel if I assumed that you wanted to be hugged super tightly when you were angry, when what you really wanted was some personal space?

   ○ *Talking points:* We might be right when we make assumptions, but we also might be wrong. When we're wrong, we risk accidentally making a friend feel unseen, uncared for, or disrespected. That's why it's important to ask clarification questions like "What kind of flower?" or "What kind of ice cream?" or "What would help you feel better right now?"

- If you ask a friend to play together during recess and they say yes, what can you do to find out what "playing together during recess" means to them?

  - *Talking points:* You can directly ask what it means to them. You can ask yes-or-no questions like "Would you like to play tag?" or "Do you want to try the jungle gym?" You can also ask open-ended questions like "What are you in the mood to play right now?" or "What would you like to do today?"

"Part of navigating desires and boundaries, or practicing consent, is recognizing that we might not have all the answers, and we can always learn more by asking for more details before or during an interaction."

Step 4   Activity

"The details make a difference. Sometimes, adjusting just one detail can make the difference between a yes and a no. Right now, we're going to focus on the details of who, what, where, and when."

Create a table on the board that looks like this:

Who	What	Where	When
Grandparent	Hug	School	Happy

"If your **grandparent** wanted to give you a **hug** at **school** when you were feeling **happy**, would you probably say yes to a hug from them? Raise your hand if you would probably say yes."

Replace "Hug" with "Kiss on the cheek" so the chart on your board looks like the one below.

Who	What	Where	When
Grandparent	Kiss on the cheek	School	Happy

"What if your **grandparent** wanted to give you a **kiss on the cheek** at **school** when you were feeling **happy**? Raise your hand if you would probably say yes to that."

Continue on, replacing certain details of the scenario. Each time, take a poll to learn how students' answers change.

- For the next one, replace *Grandparent* with *Parent*.

- Then replace *School* with *Home*.

- And last, replace *Happy* with *Annoyed*.

DISCUSSION QUESTIONS:

- Based on this exercise, why might providing details help someone make decisions that feel good?

  - *Talking points:* Details can make a big difference in a how a person feels and therefore how they will decide to respond.

- Thinking about how the class reacted to these different scenarios, what are some reasons a person might say no to a hug from someone they love or care about or to playing a game with someone they love or care about?

  - *Talking points:* A person might say no to someone they love because of where they are or how they're feeling. When someone says no, they're not saying no to you as a person, they're saying no to your request right here, right now.

- Based on this exercise, do you think it's okay to assume that because your sibling said yes to borrowing their game at home today, they're okay with you borrowing their game at home tomorrow?

  - *Talking points:* You can't be sure if they're okay with it unless you ask. That being said, you can also set up a general rule. You might have a conversation with them where you ask if it's okay to borrow their game when they're not home or if it's okay to borrow their game if they're not using it. Of course, they can always change their mind (more on this in lesson 4.4), but just like asking first is a strategy for navigating your desires and their boundaries, setting up a general rule is also a strategy for doing so.

- Based on this exercise, do you think it's okay to assume that because your sibling said yes to borrowing their game at home, they're okay with you borrowing their game at school?

  - *Talking points:* Same as the previous.

Model It

- Ask clarifying questions about the who, what, where, and when.

  - This will model for them how to integrate these kinds of questions into their requests, invitations, and negotiations.

  - Pair this with a reminder for the student to check in with their body. Give them a chance to practice noticing what they want and what they are comfortable with.

  - Even when we do our best to gather more details and ask clarifying questions, we still might end up making assumptions that create conflict. When this happens, we need to acknowledge our role. In a situation between you and another student, you might say something like "Oh, I didn't think to ask what color you wanted me to use. I'll try to remember to next time." In coaching students through conflict, you might offer, "Brandon, when you said you would combine all of the pieces of the presentation, you meant that you would put them all into one computer file. Nikha, it sounds like you thought Brandon would combine all of the pieces and work on them to make them match. There were some details missing about what you each understood Nikha's role to be." From here, you can offer, "Can you see what information was missing?" or "What might we do now to resolve this?" or "What can we take from this for next time?" We'll go more into what repair looks like in moments like these in module 5.

Coach It

- Prompt students to consider relevant details.

  - When you hear students negotiating roles for a group project or creating teams and rules for a new game, you can support them with questions like "And when does each person need to have their part done by?" and "Is everyone in agreement about this?" and "Are there rules about where on the body you're allowed to touch someone during this game of tag? Is everyone on board with that?" Questions like these will help students put their assumptions out in the open and clarify the details so that everyone more fully knows the interests and limits of others, as well as what they are agreeing to.

MODULE 3

I Listen
to Their
Response

Their Body Talks to Me

Learning Objectives:

By the end of this lesson, students will be able to:

1. Define *body language*.

2. Demonstrate an awareness of how body language plays a role in their everyday interactions.

3. Identify the implications of common body language cues.

4. Differentiate between *relying* on body language and *incorporating* body language in their interpersonal interactions.

5. Demonstrate an awareness of how tone of voice can impact interpretations and how they can check in on their assumptions.

Materials:

- Whiteboard
- Whiteboard markers

Before You Start:

- Read through the lesson plan.

Time: 35 minutes

Step 1   Introduce the Topic

Guide the class in taking two deep breaths.

"Now that we've talked about how to get in touch with what you want and ask for it in a kind and caring way, we're going to shift our focus. In the coming lessons, we're going to explore how to interpret, or make sense of, a friend's response. We're going to talk about yeses and noes and everything in between. Today's topic is understanding body language."

Ask the class if they are familiar with what body language is.

Expand on their responses: "*Body language* describes how bodies communicate without speaking words. In an earlier lesson (lesson 2.1), we discovered how each of our bodies talks to us to tell us how it's feeling. Similarly, other people's bodies can talk to us and give us information about how they're feeling too.

"When it comes to body language, sometimes we move our bodies on purpose to convey something (or say something) without words. For example, we might intentionally put our arms out for a hug. But sometimes our bodies move and convey something without us even realizing it. For example, we might widen our eyes because we are feeling surprised."

Ask the class if anyone has a pet at home. Then ask the students who are pet owners to share how they know if their animals do or don't like something. Emphasize that even though animals cannot talk, we can still get a sense of how they are feeling and what they might want based on their body language.

Explain the importance of using both verbal and nonverbal cues when practicing consent: "We're better at practicing consent when we pay attention to friends' words *and* their body language."

Step 2 Discussion

Read the following scenario: "Ella and Marquis are best friends. One day, they decide to play catch. Ella has the ball and is ready to toss it to Marquis."

DISCUSSION QUESTIONS:

- What might Marquis be doing with his body to tell Ella that he's ready to catch the ball?

  - *Talking points:* He might have his hands out, be making eye contact, and be facing forward. If students say things like "paying attention," ask them to describe what paying attention looks like.

- What might happen if Ella throws the ball when Marquis isn't ready?

  - *Talking points:* Marquis might get hurt, Marquis might get frustrated at Ella, or Ella might get frustrated at Marquis for not paying attention. Paying attention to body language can play a big role in helping situations go smoothly.

- What can Ella do if Marquis says he's ready but he seems distracted?

  - *Talking points:* Ella can double-check his answer, Ella can ask for eye contact, or Ella can point out what they notice that's leading them to believe Marquis isn't actually ready (e.g., "Your hands aren't up so I just wanted to double-check").

Reinforce the way that paying attention to another person's body language can help us navigate our choices.

Step 3   Activity

The following activity is called Act It Out. You can act out the body language described next or invite students to do so. Similar to charades, someone will act out the feeling or scenario listed. Call on students to guess what the actor is doing or communicating. Each scenario comes with hints that can help you or students act it out. The purpose of the activity is to help students recognize how they intentionally or unintentionally communicate with their body language. Remember, no talking!

Explain the instructions to the class and then begin.

- **Scenario 1:** Feeling upset

    ○ *Suggestion:* Put your hands on your hips and make a mad face (furrow your eyebrows and purse your lips).

- **Scenario 2:** Waiting or feeling impatient

    ○ *Suggestion:* Imagine you're wearing a watch. Look at your wrist (where the watch would be) and, with your other hand, tap that spot on your wrist with your finger a few times in a row. Then look up at the class with your eyes widened.

- **Scenario 3:** Wanting a student to hand you something

    ○ *Suggestion:* Approach a student's desk. Stand next to it and look at something on their desk and then put your hand out.

- **Scenario 4:** Feeling cold

    ○ *Suggestion:* Cross your arms across your chest and stroke the tops of your arms. Take a breath in through your nose, cup your hands around your mouth, and breathe out through your mouth.

DISCUSSION QUESTIONS:

- How did that feel? Was it easy to understand what the actor was communicating? Why or why not?

    ○ *Talking points:* Prompt students to consider what makes them feel confident or unsure when interpreting someone else's body language.

- What can you do if you're not sure what a person's body language is trying to tell you?
  - *Talking points:* Ask!
- In the scenario where the actor was waiting and feeling impatient, they were doing things on purpose to show impatience (for the purpose of this activity). Is it possible for you to show impatience without realizing?
  - *Talking points:* Yes. You might shake your leg, space out, or look frustrated without even meaning to. We can learn a lot from body language that's not done on purpose, *and* we can't always know whether body language is on purpose or not.
- Is it possible for you to feel impatient but not show it?
  - *Talking points:* Yes. Sometimes we try to purposely change our body language to hide our feelings. (From here you can ask why someone might change their body language on purpose and reinforce why it's important to give people space for their feelings and not just rely on body language cues or on the absence of certain body language cues).
- In the scenario where the actor was using body language to show that they were cold, is it fair to say they wanted a sweater? Why or why not?
  - *Talking points:* Discuss the difference between recognizing how someone probably feels and what they want: "If someone is cold, they might want a sweater, but they might just want the fan turned off or maybe a hug for body heat. We can offer these options. However, to wrap someone in a sweater or hug someone because they're shivering might actually make them uncomfortable. Recognizing body language is just one part of communication." You can use the example of the person being mad, too: "In the scenario where the actor was mad, is it fair to say they wanted a hug to feel better? Why or why not? What else might you offer them?"

Step 4   Activity + Discussion

"Now we're going to explore some specific body language signals or cues that might tell us how someone is feeling during an interaction."

Do this activity as a class. Read out each body language cue one by one, and then demonstrate it. Instruct students to indicate whether they believe that the cue shows that the person is probably enjoying the interaction or probably not enjoying the interaction by showing a thumbs-up or thumbs-down, respectively. A thumb in the middle means "I'm not sure" or "I can't decide."

As students give their answers, you can ask them why they put a thumb up or thumb down. For most of these, there's no right answer.

- Smiling
- Giving eye contact
- Antsy legs
- Quickened breathing
- Looking away

- Actively participating
- Eyebrows furrowing
- Leaning toward you
- Sweaty palms

- Sneering
- Tense shoulders
- Half smiling
- Slowed breathing

As you move down the list, you'll notice students disagreeing about what a certain cue indicates, and many will be undecided about what a certain cue means. Students will also likely point out that a single cue can have many meanings. This is what we want students to recognize!

DEBRIEF:

"A single body language cue can often have more than one meaning. People cry when they're sad, but people also cry when they're overcome with happiness. When paying attention to body language, it's important that we focus not just on one cue, but on the *entire* language their body is speaking. If they're crying, are they also smiling? Or are they looking away? We don't want to use one body language cue to decide for them how *they* feel. And most importantly, when we're not sure what a body language signal or cue means, we can ask them."

Write these questions on the board:

- "Is that a happy cry or a sad cry?"

- "I see you looking away. Are you okay?"

- "When my breathing slows, it's usually because I'm nervous. Is that what it means for you right now?"

Then ask the class if they can think of other ways that they can use their words to check in on someone's body language.

Close this activity by sharing, "Before we move on, it's important to mention that different body language cues can have different meanings depending on the culture or place that you're in (e.g., in the United States, a head nod means yes, while in India, some head nods can mean no), but those meanings might not be universal. This is why we must take care when communicating with others and when talking about how we communicate."

"In our last activity today, we're going to be talking about *how* we say things. The tone of voice we use when we communicate with others can affect how they hear our message. Communication is not just about *what* you say but also about *how* you say it."

Write the sentence *I'm going to school today* on the board. Then, one by one, call out the feelings listed after this paragraph. Invite students to say, in unison, "I'm going to school today" using a tone of voice to represent that feeling.

FEELINGS:

- Happy
- Scared
- Serious
- Sad
- Surprised
- Joking
- Angry

When you've gone through the whole list, ask the class how the sentence's meaning changes when they change their tone. Prompt them to give specific examples.

Then, do the same activity with the word *no*. As you call each feeling out, invite students to say no aloud in a tone of voice that represents that feeling.

DISCUSSION QUESTIONS:

- What can you do if someone says no but their tone of voice sounds like they're joking? For example, you ask them if they mind if you poke them and they say a no that sounds like they're joking.

  - *Talking points:* Double-check if their no is a playful no or a real no. Without checking in on what they mean, a no needs to be interpreted as no and saying stop needs to be interpreted as stop. This is also a great time to establish a safe word. If you're doing something like having a pillow fight, it might be fun to say "No!" and "Ah!" and "Stop!" even though you're having fun and don't want them to stop. A safe word is a word that means "I actually need you to stop." If our safe word is *pineapple*, we can be silly and pretend to be scared or struggling as we say things like no and stop. But once someone says "pineapple," it means everyone actually has to stop, check in, see what needs to be done, and handle the situation from there.

- What can you do if someone says yes but their tone of voice is nervous or scared?

  - *Talking points:* Double-check how they're feeling. Remind them that it's okay for them to say no.

Model It

- Name body language you observe.

  - Model for your students how you observe body language and incorporate it into what you choose to ask, say, or do next. You might share with the class, "I'm noticing there is a lot of fidgeting right now and not many raised hands. How does a movement break sound?"

  - In observing a conflict between peers, you might reflect, "I see crossed arms and frustrated faces. What's going on?" Say what you notice out loud.

- Take note of your body language.

  - Because there's a range of meaning behind different body language cues and facial expressions, people around you might misinterpret your body language. Does your curious face look like a face of judgment? Does your pay-attention face look like you're completely zoned out? Are your arms crossed while a student is sharing something personal and difficult?

  - Pay attention to your body language and make adjustments, or even call out what is happening with your body, to support an interaction. If you notice that you're feeling frustrated because students are struggling to pay attention or being loud and rowdy, you can say something like "I feel my jaw clenching and my body getting antsy. I'm starting to get frustrated. I'm going to pause and take a deep breath." Demonstrate how you incorporate body language into creating healthier social interactions.

Coach It

- Prompt students to pay attention to body language.

  - In the same vein, instead of saying "I see crossed arms and frustrated faces. What's going on?," you might prompt a student by asking "What do you notice about Imani's body language right now? What is it telling you? Do you think they want to be play-wrestled right now?" This can be a really helpful start to conflict resolution.

They Say Yes

Learning Objectives:

By the end of this lesson, students will be able to:

1. Navigate scenarios in which a person's level of interest is ambiguous.

2. Compare the feelings of wanting, willing, and enduring.

3. Recognize when another person is wanting, willing, or enduring.

4. Identify various situations in which they personally are wanting, willing, or enduring.

Time: 40 minutes

Materials:

- Worksheet 3.2.1

- Worksheet 3.2.2

- Red, yellow, and green paper (amount depends on which option you choose in step 2)

- Tape (if you choose option 2 in step 2)

- Whiteboard

- Whiteboard markers

Before You Start:

- Read through the lesson plan.

- Decide which option in step 2 best suits your class. Cut up pieces of red, yellow, and green paper or put aside one piece each of red, yellow, and green paper (and tape), accordingly.

- Print worksheet 3.2.1 (one per student).

- Print worksheet 3.2.2 (one per student).

Step 1 Introduce the Topic

Guide the class in taking two deep breaths.

"Today, we're going to focus on yeses. We're going to look at what it means when someone says yes and the difference between a wanting yes and a willing yes."

Write the following on the board:

> Dad: "Want a hug?"
>
> Alec: "Yeah, okay."

Have a student read the phrases. Then ask the class:

- "How much does Alec want a hug from their dad? What makes you say that?"

- "Is it hard to tell? Why or why not?"

After hearing some responses, introduce students to the concept of different kinds of yeses: "Some yeses are enthusiastic, like an excited and full-hearted, 'Yes! That sounds awesome!' Some yeses are more neutral, or unenthusiastic, like Alec's 'Yeah, okay.' Both kinds of yeses are yeses, *and* when you hear a not-so-full-hearted yes, it can be helpful to pause and check in so that you can better understand that person's desires and boundaries.

"To demonstrate what this might look like in your own lives, we're going to play a game where your job is to help the characters Asha and Ravi figure out if sharing a hug right now would be practicing good consent."

This game can be played one of two ways. Decide which option best suits your class and then introduce the rules.

- **Option 1:** For this option, students stay seated. Each student gets one piece of red paper, one piece of yellow paper, and one piece of green paper. You will read each of the following scenarios one by one, and students will indicate what they understand to be true about the situation.

    - Holding up the red paper means you believe a hug isn't a good idea because Ravi's and Asha's boundaries and desires don't match up.

    - Holding up the yellow paper means you believe Ravi should slow down and check in before going in for a hug because there's more that the two of them need to navigate.

    - Holding up the green paper means you believe Ravi and Asha are all systems go—their boundaries and desires align!

- **Option 2:** This option requires enough room for students to move around. Hang a piece of red paper in one area of the room, a piece of yellow paper in a separate area, and a piece of green paper in a third area. Rather than holding up a piece of paper, students will move to the area of the room that corresponds to their assessment of the situation.

STATEMENTS:

1. Ravi asks Asha for a hug, and she says, "No thanks."

2. Ravi asks Asha for a hug, and she says an excited yes.

3. Ravi asks Asha for a hug, and Asha shrugs.

4. Ravi asks Asha for a hug, and she says, "Maybe later."

5. Ravi tells Asha "I just *have* to give you a hug." Asha doesn't say anything.

6. Ravi tells Asha "I just *have* to give you a hug." Asha says, "I would love that."

7. Ravi hugs Asha without asking.

8. Ravi asks Asha for a hug. She smiles and looks away.

9. Ravi hugs Asha and says, "They were hugging you, so I'm gonna hug you too."

Regardless of which option you choose, when there is disagreement within the class, ask students to share why they answered the way they did. Conclude the activity with the following discussion questions.

DISCUSSION QUESTIONS:

- Why might someone say yes to a hug (or anything else) in a neutral or unenthusiastic way?

    ○ *Talking points:* They might be okay with a hug but not really *want* it, they might feel too nervous to say no, they might feel bad saying no, or they might be distracted or not really paying attention.

- What kind of check-in questions might you want to ask someone whose yes isn't enthusiastic?

    ○ *Talking points:* "You seem not so excited. Are you sure?" or "Remember, any answer you give is okay," or "I feel like maybe you don't really want a hug. Am I picking up on something that you're feeling?"

"Checking in on a friend's yes is a great way to get a sense of whether or not they're actually on board with the plan. We're going to learn some language to help make these kinds of check-ins feel smooth and give you the important information you need.

"Imagine that you and your friend Jo spent a long and busy day together. You're hungry and talking about what you want for dinner."

Ask a couple of students to share what they might choose for dinner after a long, busy day.

Continue the scenario: "You get home to find out you're not having your top-choice food. Instead, you're having macaroni and cheese for dinner. It's what your sister requested." [If a student picked macaroni and cheese as the food they would want, fill this in with a different popular food.]

"You're hungry and okay with having macaroni and cheese for dinner, but it turns out that Jo has food sensitivities to the ingredients in mac and cheese. They don't have a major allergy, but mac and cheese always upsets their stomach. Jo is feeling nervous and decides that instead of speaking up, they're going to eat with your family and deal with the digestive consequences to come."

Write the phrases *want to*, *willing to*, and *enduring* on the board. Ask the class, "Who in this scenario is eating what they *want* to eat? Who is eating what they are *willing* to eat? Who is *enduring* what they are eating?" (You will define *enduring* in a moment.)

Once students have correctly categorized the sister as "want to," themselves as "willing to," and Jo as "enduring," ask them how they knew this and how they would define these terms. Then share the following definitions on the board (Martin & Dalzen, 2021):

- *Want to:* It's what you want. It's your top choice.

- *Willing to:* It's not your top choice, but you are fully willing because someone else wants it and has chosen it.

- *Enduring:* You are tolerating or putting up with it; you are beyond what you are okay with.

"Given what we've discussed today, why might your sister give a more enthusiastic or excited yes to macaroni and cheese than you would?" Invite students to share their answers. Connect their responses to the concepts of wanting and willing.

Step 4   Activity

"Let's examine these concepts more closely." Introduce worksheet 3.2.1. Allow students five minutes to complete the worksheet and then review the answers as a class. Spend time clarifying where there is confusion. You can also do this activity as a class.

It's okay if an answer is not clear or there's disagreement. This is exactly the point. Communication is hard. If you're not sure how someone is feeling about an activity or choice, you can ask them and dig deeper.

Step 5   Activity

"Now let's revisit the Who, What, Where, and When activity with these concepts in mind and get a sense of our own individual want to, willing to, and enduring feelings. Instead of just sharing whether you're a yes or a no, I want you to consider whether you would probably be a want to, a willing to, or an enduring."

Rewrite the following table on the board.

Introduce worksheet 3.2.2 to the class. Review the instructions and refresh students' memories about this activity.

Who	What	Where	When
Grandparent	Hug	School	Happy

"If your grandparent suggested a hug at school when you were feeling happy, would you want that and choose that for yourself, would you be wholeheartedly willing to allow a hug if that's what they wanted, or would you feel like saying yes would be beyond what you are okay with?

"Would you need any other details to decide which category you would fall into? These are the questions that you'll be answering on this worksheet." Give students three minutes to complete the worksheet. You can also do this activity together as a class like you did in the first Who, What, Where, and When activity.

DISCUSSION QUESTIONS:

- Was it helpful for you to differentiate between want to, willing to, and enduring (instead of just between yes and no)?
  - *Talking points:* There's no right answer. Students may or may not find this tool helpful.

- What are some ways to find out if saying yes will lead you to a feeling of enduring?

  - *Talking points:* Pause to notice your body, find out more details about what the activity involves, or maybe try it out by starting small (e.g., try part of the plan and check in after a minute, or if it's a hug, ask for a side hug or light squeeze).

- Can you always know ahead of time whether a choice you make will feel like you're enduring?

  - *Talking points:* We don't know. That's why it's important to not just "get" or "give" a yes but to make sure that throughout the interaction, you're paying attention to your boundaries and desires and supporting others in noticing and speaking up for their boundaries and desires.

- Is it possible to start out as wanting or willing but then end up in a place where you're enduring? Does anyone have an example of this?

  - *Talking points:* Yes. Think about a time where you said yes and enjoyed it but then had enough and didn't like it anymore. We'll talk more about how minds change in a future lesson (lesson 4.4).

Supporting This Lesson in Your Classroom's Culture

Model It

- Use the language of want to, willing to, and enduring in your decision-making. It can help you get a sense of where you can be flexible and where you really can't be.

  - You may want to start off the day with a math worksheet, but if a student suggests their favorite math game, are you willing to make that adjustment? There's no correct answer across the board. The "right" answer will depend on answers to questions like: How will doing so impact the rest of the learning and the rest of the day? Is there a unanimous desire to do a math game instead? Do you have the capacity to lead this math game first thing in the morning? We'll talk more about collaboration later, but this is a great way to start getting a feel for where you are mostly making decisions for students and where you are including students in the decision-making.

  - Students might use the language of enduring to refuse a request. We'll talk more about this in the next lesson. This is also when collaboration comes in. We'll introduce collaboration in lesson 3.5 and review how to handle situations like this in that lesson.

Coach It

- When students say "But they said yes . . . ," remind them that a yes doesn't have magical power.

    ○ Someone might say yes because it's something they actually want to do. Someone might say yes because it's something they are willing to do. Someone might say yes because saying no is hard for them. People can also give a yes that later becomes a no. Another person might say yes and realize they only said yes because they misunderstood what they were saying yes to. We're going to talk in depth about all of these scenarios later.

    ○ For now, the key is to help kids understand that a yes doesn't always mean "they wanted to." Already we've seen two types of yeses: (1) a yes about what *you* want (want to) and (2) a yes about what *others* want (willing to). So often, we assume that someone's yes means that they *wanted* to do something, but it's not accurate or fair to the reality of the situation and the people around us to do so. A person might say yes because they *wanted* to or they might say yes because they were *willing* to. You can support students who are experiencing conflict by reminding them of this.

Worksheet 3.2.1

Directions: Read each of the statements provided. Consider whether the person is feeling "want to," "willing to," or "enduring." Circle your answer.

Remember:*

- **Want to** means it's your top choice. You believe it will bring you joy.
- **Willing to** means it's not your top choice, but you are fully willing because someone else wants it and has chosen it.
- **Enduring** means you are tolerating or putting up with it; you are beyond what you are okay with.

1. I want to play Monopoly.	*Want to*	*Willing to*	*Enduring*
2. I'm willing to go to your house tonight.	*Want to*	*Willing to*	*Enduring*
3. If it were up to me, we'd order sushi for dinner.	*Want to*	*Willing to*	*Enduring*
4. I'm not okay with hugs.	*Want to*	*Willing to*	*Enduring*
5. I'd love a shoulder massage.	*Want to*	*Willing to*	*Enduring*
6. We can play hide-and-seek now.	*Want to*	*Willing to*	*Enduring*
7. If you hug me, I'll be super upset.	*Want to*	*Willing to*	*Enduring*
8. I'll braid your hair if you'll braid mine after.	*Want to*	*Willing to*	*Enduring*
9. I'm okay with going to the pool.	*Want to*	*Willing to*	*Enduring*
10. That's a great idea. I'd be happy to join you.	*Want to*	*Willing to*	*Enduring*
11. You chose a movie without checking with me. I'm terrified of horror movies.	*Want to*	*Willing to*	*Enduring*

---

* These definitions are adapted from *The Art of Receiving and Giving: The Wheel of Consent* (Martin & Dalzen, 2021).

Worksheet 3.2.2

Directions: Look at each scenario and indicate whether you would probably be a want to, a willing to, or an enduring by shading in the box that best describes how you would feel. If there are other details you would need to consider in making your decision, write those down beneath each example (e.g., "I would be willing to if it were their birthday" or "I would be enduring if it was the grandparent I don't know well").

1. Your <u>grandparent</u> suggests a <u>hug</u> at <u>school</u> when you are feeling <u>happy</u>.

That's something I would **want to** do and would choose for myself.	That's something I would be **willing to** do if that's what they wanted.	That's something I would be **enduring** and it would be beyond what I'm okay with.

2. Your <u>grandparent</u> suggests a <u>kiss on the cheek</u> at <u>school</u> when you are feeling <u>happy</u>.

That's something I would **want to** do and would choose for myself.	That's something I would be **willing to** do if that's what they wanted.	That's something I would be **enduring** and it would be beyond what I'm okay with.

3. Your <u>parent</u> suggests a <u>kiss on the cheek</u> at <u>school</u> when you are feeling <u>happy</u>.

That's something I would **want to** do and would choose for myself.	That's something I would be **willing to** do if that's what they wanted.	That's something I would be **enduring** and it would be beyond what I'm okay with.

4. Your <u>parent</u> suggests a <u>kiss on the cheek</u> at <u>home</u> when you are feeling <u>happy</u>.

That's something I would **want to** do and would choose for myself.	That's something I would be **willing to** do if that's what they wanted.	That's something I would be **enduring** and it would be beyond what I'm okay with.

5. Your <u>parent</u> suggests a <u>kiss on the cheek</u> at <u>home</u> when you are <u>annoyed</u>.

That's something I would **want to** do and would choose for myself.	That's something I would be **willing to** do if that's what they wanted.	That's something I would be **enduring** and it would be beyond what I'm okay with.

They Say No

Time:
40 minutes

Learning Objectives:

By the end of this lesson, students will be able to:

1. Describe the difference between being a guardian of someone's boundaries and ignoring someone's boundaries.

2. Describe why it's important to respond to a no with kindness.

3. Respond to a no with kindness.

4. Identify coping strategies for dealing with the hard emotions that might accompany a no.

Materials:

- Worksheet 3.3.1
- Worksheet 3.3.2
- Whiteboard
- Whiteboard markers
- Flip chart paper (optional)

Before You Start:

- Read through the lesson plan.
- Print worksheet 3.3.1 (one per student).
- Print worksheet 3.3.2 (one per student).
- Draw the table in step 3 on the board. Cover it with flip chart paper.
- Decide how you will pair up students in step 4.

Step 1   Introduce the Topic

Guide the class in taking two deep breaths.

"Last time, we spoke about what you need to consider when you make a request and the other person says yes. Today, we're going to talk about what to do when you make a request and the other person says no.

"What are some ways a person might say no or indicate that they're not interested in doing what you suggested?"

Create a list with their answers on the board.

"There are a lot of ways to say no. In some moments, saying no can be more challenging than we might think. We're going to dive into that later. For now, we're going to focus on the experience of someone saying no to you, of *hearing* a no."

Step 2   Discussion

Introduce worksheet 3.3.1 to the class and review the instructions. Remind them that this worksheet is for their eyes only. Give students about five minutes to complete the worksheet.

Ask students how a person might feel when they hear a no. Their answers can be based on the memory they shared on the worksheet or on other experiences. Students will often list emotions such as anger, sadness, disappointment, and embarrassment.

As students share their stories and feelings, reinforce the themes you hear students repeating.

DISCUSSION QUESTIONS:

- Is bad to feel these difficult emotions?

    ○ *Talking points:* No. It's totally normal and healthy to feel these emotions. The key is what we do with these emotions. We need to make sure our feelings don't get the best of us and lead us to say hurtful things or do hurtful things.

- If saying no feels frustrating or sad for the other person, does this mean that we shouldn't say no?

    ○ *Talking points:* No. We need to be honest about our boundaries and limits. It's okay to feel hard things. Part of being a good friend means being able to give space for the other person to say yes *or* no.

Point to the table you drew on the board.

	Be a guardian of their boundaries	**Ignore their boundaries**
What it looks like	Listening for what they are and are not comfortable with Not pushing them beyond their limits	Focusing on your desires even though this is outside the other person's comfort level Pressuring someone else into changing their decision
What it sounds like	"Cool, no worries." "All right, thanks for telling me." "Okay."	"If you were really my friend, you would do this." "If you don't do this, I'm going to tell everyone that gossip you told me."

Review the chart. Then say, "When you hear a no, you have two choices: you can be a guardian of the person's boundaries or ignore the person's boundaries. How you respond will send a message to them about whether or not you respect their limits and whether or not you respect them."

Introduce worksheet 3.3.2 to the class and review the instructions. Give students about four minutes to complete the worksheet. Once students have completed it, review the answers together. Check in to see if students have any questions.

ANSWER KEY: 1 C, 2 E, 3 A, 4 B, 5 D

"Now it's time for practice."

In this activity, students will pair up to practice saying, hearing, and responding to a no. In each pair, one student will start as student A and one will start as student B before switching roles. Pairs can remain the same throughout each of the four rounds. While these interactions are manufactured, there are still important feelings we can examine and lessons we can learn.

If there is another teacher available, they can write the scripts on the board as you go. Otherwise, you can do so.

In round 1, instruct students to enact the following script:

Student A: "Can I have a hug?"

Student B: "No."

Student A: "Okay."

Then have students switch roles. When both partners have had a turn, facilitate a short debrief. Ask students how it felt to hear an okay in response to their no. Prompt them to use feeling words. There are no right answers.

If students ask if they can say yes, let them know that you're glad they want to say yes, but for this activity, the instructions are to say no.

In round 2, instruct students to enact the following script:

Student B: "Can I have a hug?"

Student A: "No."

Student B: "Thank you for telling me that." (or some other version of "Thank you for sharing your boundaries.")

Then have students switch roles. When both partners have had a turn, facilitate a short debrief. Ask students how it felt to hear a thank-you in response to their no. There are no right answers.

In round 3, instruct students to enact the following script:

Student A: "Can I have a hug?"

Student B: "No."

Student A: "C'mon, please, you have to!" (or some other version of pressuring their friend)

Then have students switch roles. When both partners have had a turn, facilitate a short debrief. Ask students how it felt to be pressured in response to their no. There are no right answers.

In round 4, instruct students to enact the following script:

Student B: "Can I have a hug?"

Student A: "No."

Student B: "C'mon, please, you have to!" (or some other version of pressuring their friend)

Student A: "When you say _____, I hear/I feel _____."

The goal is for the student to explain to their peer how their response makes them feel (e.g., "When you say 'C'mon, please,' I feel like you're not respecting my answer" or "When you say, 'You have to,' I hear you caring about your wants but not about mine").

Then have students switch roles. When both partners have had a turn, facilitate a short debrief. Ask students how it felt to stand up for themselves in this way. There are no right answers.

Close this activity by exploring any additional thoughts or questions.

Step 5   Discussion

Introduce students to the final discussion of the lesson: "We know that hearing a no can be hard. We also know that we shouldn't let those tough feelings lead to unkind words and actions toward our friends. So, what can you do when you notice challenging emotions arise after hearing someone say no to your ask?"

Listen to students' responses and review any coping skills that you've already discussed as a class. If you haven't yet discussed coping skills together, introduce them to techniques such as deep breathing, counting to 10, talking to a teacher, journaling, positive affirmations, going on a walk, drinking water, and so on.

This is a great time to practice some of these coping skills too.

Supporting This Lesson in Your Classroom's Culture

Model It

- Befriend your students' refusals (or at least don't make an enemy out of them).

  ○ I regularly hear teachers and parents talk about how students and children have used the concept of "no means no" against them.

  ○ Here's an example of a scenario and some ways to handle it: A teacher tells a student to stop talking to their classmate. The student says, "No. It's my body, my choice. No means no."

    - *Show them that you understand their side:* Starting with something simple—like "You want to keep talking to Andrea. I get it. Andrea is awesome."—can show them that you get where they're coming from. If we're honest with ourselves, we can probably recognize why students want to talk to a friend instead of listening to us. We can show them we see that perspective.

- *Remind them of the limits of choice:* Remind the student that their body belongs to them *and* their choice only extends to where it doesn't impact other people. Right now, their voice is impacting others' learning. They're more than welcome to talk to their classmate at recess, where it won't disrupt learning. "My body is mine" is not a tool to be used as free rein to do whatever they want; it's a reminder that we have choice over our bodies, and we can make choices to consider ourselves and consider those around us.

- *Give the student options (based on the reason for their no):* Remind the student about the limits of choice *and* give them a choice. If they're talking because they're bored, you might offer them something stimulating to do quietly. If they're talking because they say they already know what you're teaching, you might have them teach with you. If they're talking because they're feeling too lost to catch up, you might invite them to write down questions they have. Consider why they might be saying no and give them other options.

- *Collaborate:* Tell the student that you understand that they want to keep talking but that it's distracting for the class and the learning. Ask the student for suggestions on how you can both move forward and feel good about what's happening. Show them that you're their teammate, not their commander. We'll discuss collaboration more in lesson 3.5.

- *Have a 1:1 conversation:* In moments like this, if you have another teacher in the room, they can also support you by having a one-to-one conversation with the student.

Coach It

- Help students see the way that boundaries are a relationship gift.

  - When a student is feeling disappointed because they heard a no, it can be so tempting to reassure the student that there's an acceptable reason for their peer's no. Perhaps you want to insist "It's okay, they're probably just tired" or "I'm sure there was a good reason for their no; try again tomorrow." But this approach doesn't support our ultimate goal of developing students' ability to be a guardian of others' boundaries. Instead of rationalizing another student's decision to say no, empathize with how the student who asked the question might be feeling. Once the student is regulated, you can try reminding them that a no is information that allows them to be in healthy relationship with their friends. The fact that a friend felt comfortable saying no says that they trust you. We don't always need to know, or get to know, why someone has said no. Our job is to hear their response and respect it.

- Use the concept "When you say _____, I hear/I feel _____."

    ○ When one student says no and the other student replies in a way that pushes against the no or tries to pressure the no into a yes, you can step in and ask questions of the student who's pushing: "Johnny, when Alex says, 'No, I'm not in the mood,' what do think he's trying to tell you?" or even "When Alex tells you, 'No, I'm not in the mood,' I hear them saying that they're not interested. Johnny, what do you hear?"

    ○ It's easy for students, and even for us, to go on autopilot and not really pay attention to how the words we say impact those around us. Drawing attention to the meaning behind the words can help students be more thoughtful about what they say.

Worksheet 3.3.1

Directions: Have you ever had a friend say no to your invitation for an after-school playdate or hang? A parent decide that you don't get to have dessert? A classmate ignore your idea for the group project? Or a sibling choose to read a book by themselves instead of playing a game with you?

Share your experience in the space below. Describe how you felt in that moment. How did it feel to have someone say no to giving you what you wanted or doing what you wanted? Remember to use feeling words.

Worksheet 3.3.2

How you respond to a person's no will tell that person how you feel about their right to their boundaries.

Directions: Draw a line to match each stated phrase with the message it conveys.

1. "Do you want to do something else instead?"

2. "Please, please, please, please."

3. "I promise you're gonna have fun."

4. "It's not a big deal, just do it."

5. "Oh, gotcha!"

A. I know how you'll feel better than you do.

B. Instead of listening to yourself, listen to me.

C. I want both of us to have fun.

D. I accept your answer.

E. I'm going to wear you down until I get what I want.

What If They Say Maybe?

Time: 20 minutes

Learning Objectives:

By the end of this lesson, students will be able to:

1. Demonstrate how to treat an answer that's not a full-on yes.

2. Describe why someone might say maybe when they really want to say yes or say no.

Materials:

- Worksheet 3.4.1
- Worksheet 3.4.2
- Whiteboard
- Whiteboard markers
- Flip chart paper (optional)

Before You Start:

- Read through the lesson plan.
- Print worksheet 3.4.1 (one per student).
- Print worksheet 3.4.2 (one per student).
- Decide how you will pair up students in step 3.

Step 1   Introduce the Topic

Guide the class in taking two deep breaths.

"We've explored some aspects of hearing yeses and noes, but what do you do when a friend responds to your desire, request, or offer with a maybe or 'I'm not sure'? Today, we're going to focus on this question."

Step 2 Activity

Poll the class: "Imagine you want to take a book home from the class library. You ask me if that's okay, and I say maybe. Do you have permission to take the book home?"

Invite students to share their reasoning.

Then ask the class, "By a show of hands, who here has ever said (or heard someone else say), 'But they didn't say no' as an excuse for doing something you probably weren't supposed to do?"

Reinforce that while it's tempting to use this loophole as a way to get what we want, the absence of a no isn't a yes. We don't have a right to assume that a lack of no (or not hearing no) means yes.

Introduce worksheet 3.4.1 to the class and review the instructions. Give students about three minutes to complete the worksheet. Once students have completed the worksheet, review it together.

Ask the class, "Is it ever challenging to understand whether someone is saying maybe, yes, or no?" Bring in past conversations about body language and tone of voice to discuss what you can do if you're not sure how to interpret someone's response.

Step 3 Activity + Discussion

For the following activity, split the class into pairs or groups of three. Instruct them to answer the questions on worksheet 3.4.2 together. Give students about five minutes to complete the worksheet. Once students have completed the worksheet, review their answers together.

As students share their answers, review the following:

- A person might say a genuine maybe because they need more information or details, or they need time to consider how they feel.

- A person might say maybe when they really want to say no because they feel bad saying no.

- A person might say maybe when they really want to say yes because they feel embarrassed about saying yes.

DISCUSSION QUESTION:

- What can you do when someone says maybe?

    ◦ *Talking points:*

        – If you think they are saying maybe because they feel bad saying no → remind them that no isn't mean, it's just information.

        – If you think they need time to consider how they feel → allow them the time and space to decide. Ask the class, "Have you ever made a decision you didn't feel good about because you felt pressured to make a decision quickly?"

            • If they need more information/details → provide them with missing information/details: "What information or details might a person need?"

            • "Most importantly, know that a maybe doesn't mean 'convince me.' It can be really tempting to see a maybe as an opportunity to convince someone to say yes. But as a guardian of others' boundaries, your role is to support friends as they come to their own answers that feel true to them."

Supporting This Lesson in Your Classroom's Culture

Model It

- Model your maybe when you are making decisions.

    ◦ When students make requests or share desires, take a moment to slow down. Speak your decision-making process aloud. Ask for more time to think, collect more details, or share with students why you're neither a solid yes nor a solid no.

    ◦ If a student is making their case while you sit on your maybe, you can help them distinguish between what feels like pushing to you and what feels like them giving you more information. We'll talk about this more later on too.

Coach It

- Celebrate the maybe.

    ◦ In US culture, we're often rushed to move quickly. But moving quickly means we too easily move past maybe. Since saying yes is usually easier than saying no, pushing past maybe often leads to people agreeing to do things they're not actually comfortable doing.

- Imagine a student who's having a hard time deciding whether they want to play in a group game during recess. If others are feeling frustrated that the student isn't making a decision, coach the students through or model how this can be resolved. You can ask the student if they need more time or information. Perhaps something else would sound better to them. You can remind the student that they have other options. Of course, you don't want a game to be held up because a student can't make a decision. Recess is limited. Maybe you suggest the student watch a round of the game first before deciding. This is also a great time to remind students that they can change their decision. We'll talk more about this later.

Worksheet 3.4.1

Directions: Look at the phrases below. Circle the ✓ if you think the phrase gives you permission. Circle the X if you think the phrase means you do not have permission.

I'm not sure.	✓ / X
Definitely!	✓ / X
Nah.	✓ / X
Silence	✓ / X
That sounds great.	✓ / X
I don't know.	✓ / X
That's not my thing.	✓ / X
I'm not into that.	✓ / X
Maybe.	✓ / X
Let's wait.	✓ / X
Totally!	✓ / X
I'm not up for that today.	✓ / X
Nods	✓ / X
I would love that.	✓ / X
Not right now.	✓ / X
I don't think so.	✓ / X

Worksheet 3.4.2

Directions: Working together, write down as many answers as you can to the following question:

Why might someone say maybe?

Think about times in the past when you've answered someone with a maybe. If it helps, consider why someone might say maybe to a sleepover, to play-wrestling, to a hug, or to partnering up on a project. In those moments, why might someone say maybe?

Collaboration

Time:
30 minutes

Learning Objectives:

By the end of this lesson, students will be able to:

1. Define *collaboration*.
2. Describe how to collaborate effectively in different situations.
3. Demonstrate how to collaborate with classmates on a decision.
4. Describe the limits of collaboration.

Materials:

- Script 3.5.1
- Handout 3.5.1
- Whiteboard
- Whiteboard markers

Before You Start:

- Read through the lesson plan.
- Print script 3.5.1 (two copies).
- Print handout 3.5.1 (one per student).
- Decide how you will pair up students in step 4.

Step 1   Introduce the Topic

Guide the class in taking two deep breaths.

"In the last few lessons, we explored three ways a person can respond to a request or suggestion: yes, no, and maybe. It's important that we respect a person's answer in these moments, whatever it might be, *and* there is often room for collaboration within a person's answer. Today, we're going to explore what collaboration means and how you can use collaboration to create interactions that feel good for everyone involved.

"Who can tell me what it means to collaborate?" Invite students to respond and then share the following definition.

"To collaborate means to work with another person to reach a certain goal.

"When talking about the practice of consent, the goal is to create experiences that respect both people's desires and boundaries. Whether or not *collaboration* is a new word for you, you probably collaborate every day already."

Step 2 Skit + Discussion

Invite two students to volunteer to perform a short skit. If no students are interested in volunteering, you can perform the skit with another teacher. Hand each actor a copy of script 3.5.1. Decide who will play the role of Ash and who will play the role of Charlie. Call "Action" when the actors are ready. When they're done, offer a round of applause and ask the actors to return to their seats.

DISCUSSION QUESTIONS:

- How might Ash feel if Charlie insisted that they play cards?

  ○ *Talking points:* Pressured, like they didn't have choice.

- How might Ash feel if Charlie kept saying no to their suggestions without coming up with their own ideas?

  ○ *Talking points:* Tired of coming up with ideas, like Charlie isn't doing their part, like Charlie doesn't actually want to play with them.

- What can a person do to help a collaboration go well?

  ○ *Talking points:* Collaboration works well when both people:

    - Are open to possible alternatives.

    - Are honest about their desires and boundaries.

    - Participate in coming up with ideas.

    - Listen to what the other person is saying and take what is shared into account when offering alternatives.

    - Are willing to finding a solution that makes them both willing instead of agreeing only to what they're wanting to do (see lesson 3.2).

Step 3   Discussion

"Now that we know a little bit more about what goes into collaboration, we're going to explore when to use collaboration as a tool. It might surprise you, but collaboration can be used after a maybe, after a yes, *and* sometimes even after a no."

Write the following phrases on the board: *After a maybe*, *After a yes*, and *After a no*. One by one, invite students to give an example of how collaboration might show up in each of these scenarios.

Give each student a copy of handout 3.5.1 and review it together. Use the scenarios that students came up with on the whiteboard to show how the phrases on the handout can be used. (You can also come up with scenarios on your own.)

Ask the class if they have any questions or if there's anything else that they want to add to the handout.

Step 4   Practice + Discussion

In this activity, students will pair up to practice collaboration. In each pair, one student will be student A and one will be student B.

"Using Charlie and Ash as models, we're going to practice collaborating."

Explain to students how the practice will go:

1. Student A will suggest a game or movement activity.

2. Instead of just responding with a yes, no, or maybe, student B will share a need or an alternative activity, just like Ash and Charlie did. Ash suggested cards, and Charlie countered that offer by suggesting 20 Questions.

3. Both students will continue collaborating—suggesting ideas, sharing needs, and working on adjustments—until they find an activity that sounds good to both people.

4. Be creative and have fun with it!

Students can pick from options like stretching, doing jumping jacks, doing a staring contest, playing charades, playing Pictionary, and so on.

Remind students that:

- Once they agree on an idea, they'll have three minutes to actually play the game or do the activity.

- The activity they pick needs to be one that won't be disruptive to the rest of the class.

Give students about five minutes to collaborate and complete the activity of their choice.

If time allows, switch partners and do the practice again. Encourage students to respond a little differently in this round (e.g., if they easily came to an agreement the first time, maybe this time they take a little longer, and vice versa).

When students are done, invite them back to their seats and discuss the experience as a group.

DISCUSSION QUESTIONS:

- How did that feel? Would you do anything differently next time?
  - *Talking points:* Discuss how it felt to be collaborative (or how it felt to *try* to be collaborative). There's no right answer. This is a moment for students to reflect on their personal experience.

- How did you feel like your needs were reflected in the final decision?
  - *Talking points:* Sometimes collaborations go super smoothly. But sometimes collaboration can be tough! Maybe you had your heart set on a certain game or maybe you were really wanting things to go your way. It can be hard to hear a no in these moments. This is when it's helpful to remember your role in being a guardian of your boundaries and of others' boundaries.

- Do you think collaboration is always possible?
  - *Talking points:* Collaboration is only possible if both people are willing to be flexible and explore other options. There might be times when only one person is interested in collaborating. The other person might not be interested in doing an activity or playing together at all. Or maybe the other person is only willing to do the activity that's their number-one choice. Collaboration is only possible when both people are willing to collaborate.

- What can you do if you're not sure whether someone is interested in collaborating?
  - *Talking points:* Ask! Just like we reviewed in the collaboration handout, a person can ask something like "Are you interested in finding an activity [set of rules, game plan, and so on] that works for both of us?"

Model It

- Be a collaborator yourself.

  ○ Look back to lesson 3.2. You may want to start off the day with a math worksheet, but if a student suggests their favorite math game, are you willing to make that adjustment? Are you willing to collaborate to find an alternate plan? If yes, say aloud, "It sounds like you'd like to collaborate. Let's talk and figure something out." Once you've found a solution, reinforce how collaboration takes your perspective and their perspective into consideration.

  ○ Look back to lesson 3.3. If you're bumping heads (metaphorically) with a student in class, you can ask them if they're willing to collaborate. See if they can come up with suggestions on how you can both move forward and feel good about what's happening. You can also offer suggestions yourself. If you'd like to try this approach, keep in mind that if the student is too dysregulated, you might not get very far. Before you start collaborating with a disappointed student, ask them if they're willing to hear suggestions for collaboration or to come up with some alternatives themselves. Just as before, once you've found a solution, reinforce how collaboration takes your perspective and their perspective into consideration.

Coach It

- Use the idea of "Under what conditions . . ." or "How can we work together to make this work?"

  ○ So often, conflict can be solved by asking ourselves or the other person, "Under what conditions are you a yes? Under what conditions would you be comfortable with this?"

  ○ If you assign a group presentation to the class and there's a student who doesn't want to present, you might ask them, "Under what conditions would you be willing to stand up there with your group?" They might suggest that they stand there but don't say anything. They might suggest that they stand behind a classmate. They might suggest that the class promises to clap afterward.

  ○ When someone says no, it's usually because they are a no! Our job isn't to try to get students to say yes. Our job is to support students in problem-solving. Sometimes that means not forcing the issue in the moment and allowing them to sit out of the group presentation. But other times, it means working with them to find a solution that works for everyone.

- Bringing up a shared goal among students (like doing well in the class, learning, or having fun) can help remind them why collaboration might be something they want.

Script 3.5.1

ASH: Do you want to play a game?

CHARLIE: Yeah! Do you have playing cards?

ASH: I do, but I don't really want to play a card game right now.

CHARLIE: Do you know how to play 20 Questions?

ASH: I do! Want to do that?

CHARLIE: Yeah!

Handout 3.5.1

Read through the following scenarios to see how collaboration can be used after a maybe, after a yes, *and* sometimes even after a no.

	How to Collaborate	Notes
After a maybe	"Sounds like you're not sure. How can we make this work for both of us?"	Trying to convince someone isn't collaboration. They might just need more time and space to decide.
After a yes	"Cool, let's figure out the details." "Great! Let's talk about the what and the how."	Remember the flower activity in our lesson about being specific (lesson 2.4)? Clarifying details is super important. *Examples:* • "Yes" to a game → What kind of game? • "Yes" to tag →How would you like to set up the rules?
After a no	"Are you interested in working together to become a yes?" "I can offer you a different suggestion, if you're interested." "Is there something else you'd like to do or play?"	It's totally okay if someone isn't interested in collaborating. It's also okay if someone becomes a no during a collaboration.

MODULE 4

I Share My Limits

Noticing My Limits

Learning Objectives:

By the end of this lesson, students will be able to:

1. Notice how their bodies talk to them about their limits.

2. Demonstrate an awareness of how specific body parts communicate with them about their limits and needs.

3. Describe the difference between feeling something that is uncomfortable but tolerable and feeling something that is uncomfortable and intolerable.

4. Describe the importance of using the information their bodies communicate with them when it comes to making decisions.

Time:
35 minutes

Materials:

- Whiteboard
- Whiteboard markers

Before You Start:

- Read through the lesson plan.

Note: *This lesson strongly builds off lesson 2.1. Both lessons are focused on helping students notice their bodies. Lesson 2.1 is framed in terms of noticing our wants. This lesson is framed in terms of noticing our limits or boundaries.*

Step 1   Introduce the Topic

Guide the class in taking two deep breaths.

"In our last lesson, we spoke about collaboration. For collaboration to work, both people need to be in touch with their wants *and* with their limits or boundaries.

"In some of our first lessons together, we talked about how you can figure out what you want and communicate those wants. As we continue to build consent skills over the next few lessons, we're going to talk more about how to figure out what your limits and boundaries are and how to communicate them."

"Your body helps you stay healthy and well by talking to you about your limits. It doesn't speak in a language like English, Spanish, or American Sign Language. The body has its own way of speaking.

"Think about what you notice in your body when you're thirsty. How does your body tell you, or communicate with you, that you need water?" Answers may include mention of dry throat or mouth, sweating, panting, coughing, or feeling a headache.

Then say, "Exactly: your body tells you, 'This is too much. I'm not comfortable. If I don't change something, I will be beyond what I'm okay with.'

"This is where, again, we see the difference between wanting, willing, and enduring. There's the feeling of wanting water, the feeling of being genuinely willing to go without water until your next break, and the realization that if you wait any longer until you drink water, it will be beyond what you're okay with—that feeling is enduring. We want to pay attention to our bodies so that we can notice where our limits and boundaries are so that we can create more situations where we feel okay."

Write the following on the board:

- Heart
- Lungs
- Stomach
- Skin
- Muscles
- Eyes

As a class, name the ways these body parts "talk" to us throughout the day. How might these body parts tell us something about how we feel? If students come up with additional body parts, add them to the list! You can use these questions to help guide the activity:

- **Heart:** When does your heart beat more quickly or less quickly? Can you feel your heartbeat now? Is it beating especially fast? Consider how it functions when you've been running or jumping, when you're resting, when you're nervous, and when you're calm.

- **Lungs:** Think about your breathing rate. Are your breaths big and deep? Shallow and quick? What might be the reason for this? Consider what your breathing is like when you've been running or jumping, when you're resting, when you're nervous, and when you're calm.

- **Stomach:** Is your stomach making noises right now? Does it feel at rest? Does it feel like there's a pit inside? Or maybe some butterflies? What might these sensations suggest? Consider whether these sensations indicate that you're hungry, full, nervous, or calm.

- **Skin:** Are you feeling hot or cold? Is your body sweating? What might these symptoms suggest? Consider the temperature in the room as well as how nervous or calm you feel.

- **Muscles:** Is your body tense or relaxed? What muscles are tense or relaxed? Is your body antsy or calm? What might it mean if your posture is slouched? What might it mean if your shoulders are raised toward your ears? What might it mean if your leg muscles are jittery?

- **Eyes:** Are your eyes dry or watery right now? Are they getting big while your eyebrows are raised? What might your eyes be trying to tell you? Maybe you're surprised or excited. Are you looking down or away from people? What might that indicate?

"When we're trying to figure out what we need or if something sounds like a good idea, listening to the body can be really helpful!"

Step 3   Activity + Discussion

"In one of our earlier lessons (lesson 2.1), we paid attention to our bodies in response to a list of words. Now we're going to do some practice in noticing our bodies just as they are. Keeping the body parts that we just discussed in mind, close your eyes and take a moment to observe your own body.

"With your eyes closed, begin to pay attention to your breath. Breathe in through your nose and out through your nose. Big breaths in and big breaths out. Start to notice your body sitting in its chair." [*pause*]

"Then move your attention toward your stomach. [*pause*] What do you notice? Pay attention to the feeling inside." [*pause*]

"Now, move your attention away from your stomach and take a moment to check in on your muscles. [*pause*] What do you notice? Does your body feel relaxed or tense? Do you have the urge to move or stay in place?" [*pause*]

"Now, move your attention to your skin, maybe the skin of your arms or your face. [*pause*] What do you notice? Are there goosebumps? Do you feel sweat on any part of your body? Does any part of your body feel itchy?" [*pause*]

"Continue to take deep breaths and see what else you notice about your body right now." [*long pause*]

"Take the next few moments to slowly flutter your eyes open."

Invite students to share what they noticed about their bodies and what their bodies might be telling them about how they're feeling. You can prompt responses by asking students what they noticed about specific body parts.

"There is value in noticing your body without changing anything, but when you notice that you are enduring, or in a situation that is beyond what you can tolerate (or beyond what you are okay with), it's important to listen and take care of yourself.

"Based on what you noticed, is there anything your body really needs? Before you answer, consider the difference between being genuinely willing and enduring. If you're feeling hungry, are you willing to wait until snack time? If you're feeling like you need to use the bathroom, are you willing to wait for the last person to come back?

"Sometimes we are genuinely willing and sometimes we are not (and sometimes it can be tempting to say you are enduring so that you can get your way, even though it's not totally honest to do so). With this in mind, and thinking about what you've noticed in your body, think to yourself if there is anything you are enduring. Notice if there are any limits that have come up—if there is anything you are deeply no longer okay with.

"As you pay attention to this, I invite you to take a moment to show care for your body, whether you're enduring or whether there is just something that might make you feel better based on what you noticed. You can grab a drink of water, adjust how you're sitting, do a small stretch, take a big breath, or do anything else that takes just a few moments that would help you be more comfortable in this classroom while still being respectful of others."

After students return to their seats, take a class poll: "Raise your hand if you've ever been told to 'suck it up' or 'just deal with it' when you told an adult or a friend about something you needed. Maybe a parent insisted you didn't need water when you really did, or maybe a friend insisted that a movie wasn't that scary so you should keep watching." As students raise their hands, reinforce how common this is and how awful this feels.

"While it's important to notice in yourself whether you're genuinely willing to keep watching a scary movie or whether you're genuinely willing to wait for a snack, it's also so important to recognize the moments when continuing to watch that movie or waiting for that water would be overstepping your own boundaries. When you pay attention to your body, you can get a better sense of what's comfortable enough and what's too uncomfortable and honor what you notice by making decisions based on that."

"Now I have some questions that will help apply what we just learned to help us feel good in our everyday lives and create healthy relationships."

DISCUSSION QUESTIONS:

- What can you do when you're pretty sure your body is talking to you but you're not sure what it means?

  - *Talking points:* When we read other people's body language, we need to take more than just one cue into consideration. When it comes to understanding our own bodies, we do the same. We can pause to see what else we notice. Then we can make adjustments to see if that changes the feeling. For example, if you're not sure whether you're sweating because you're nervous or because you're hot, take some deep breaths to calm your body down. If that works, then feeling nervous was probably the answer! Use this moment to talk about how using coping strategies, like breathing, can be a tool to help us shift from enduring to willing. We have so many options beyond just a quick yes or no.

- What might happen if you don't take the time to notice your body's limits?

  - *Talking points:* You might end up in situations that really don't feel good to you and are potentially unsafe.

- What might happen if, after listening to your body's limits around something like hunger, thirst, or the fullness of your bladder, you decide not to do anything to change the situation?

  - *Talking points:* You probably won't feel good. (Use the terms *uncomfortable* and *dangerous* to outline the difference between not *immediately* attending to something like hunger and deciding not to do something about your hunger, or your body's other needs, for a long period of time.)

  - There's also a difference between deciding not to take care of your body in this way every once in a while and regularly deciding not to listen to how your body wants care. For example, in some religions it's tradition to fast (to not eat and sometimes not drink) on certain days. Choosing not to eat on these days, even though you notice your body is hungry, is a very different situation than choosing not to respond to your hunger cues regularly.

  - It's likely going to be uncomfortable to go without food for a day, and maybe even for an hour, but it is dangerous to eat only a little bit for many days. Although there can be good reasons to tolerate hunger for a short amount of time, there usually isn't good reason to tolerate hunger regularly or for a long time.

- ○ Remind students of the differences between willing, wanting, and enduring to support this idea too.

• What might happen if, after listening to your body's limits around being touched, you decide not to do anything to change the situation? For example, you don't want to be hugged, but your friend is hugging you. Or every time you visit your grandma, she kisses you on the cheek but you really don't like it. How will your relationship with that person be impacted?

- ○ *Talking points:* Emphasize that healthy relationships are built on respect and care for your boundaries and another person's boundaries. This means that we help keep our relationships healthy by sharing what we are and are not comfortable with. This also means that in a healthy relationship, the person will respect and care for your body boundaries. When you don't take action when your body tells you that you're uncomfortable with a specific kind of touch, you probably won't feel good in your body or in that relationship.

- ○ Review what happens when a person is always "willing to" but not "wanting to." If a person is always on the willing side, like the tree in *The Giving Tree*, but is never asked about their limits or getting what they want, the relationship won't be healthy and won't feel good.

- ○ If your students aren't familiar with abuse prevention strategies and the difference between safe and unsafe touch, please see the appendix for resources to help you share these necessary teachings with them.

• Do you think another person's body can talk to you?

- ○ *Talking points:* Refer back to lesson 3.1. A friend can support another friend's boundaries and give care to them by making them offers based on what they notice. For example, if you see that someone is shivering and they seem cold, you can ask if they are, in fact, feeling that way and offer them your sweatshirt. Practicing consent means caring for our desires and limits and others' desires and limits. Sometimes those desires and limits are very clear, known, and easily communicated, and sometimes they are not. That's why it's so important that we look out for ourselves and for each other. There's a better chance we'll get what's needed if we're looking out for others and others are looking out for us.

- Imagine that a friend tells you that they're so cold. You check in with your body and you notice that you are cold too. Should you give them your sweatshirt?

  - *Talking points:* This is a tough question. There is no right answer. Practicing consent means navigating your desires and boundaries *and* theirs. It's not wrong to keep the sweatshirt for yourself (after all, it is yours!). It's also not wrong to let your friend borrow it for some time. You can collaborate, but you don't have to. Perhaps you can each put on an arm of the sweater and be close for body heat. But if that much closeness would create an enduring situation for you (or them), you don't need to take that route. The important thing is that you're actively working to care for your limits and desires and the other person's limits and desires—and that they are doing the same.

Close the lesson by reinforcing the idea that practicing consent means all people are (1) open to *noticing* when their body is a no or needs a change *and* (2) open to hearing when the other person's body is a no or needs a change.

Supporting This Lesson in Your Classroom's Culture

Some of the following recommendations can be found in lesson 2.1 too:

Model It

- Vocalize what you notice about your body when making decisions.

  - As my nephews have grown, giving them piggyback rides has become more of a challenge. When I notice that my body is physically capable of continuing but that I will either wake up feeling sore tomorrow or will resent them for my yes, I will tell them what I notice in my body and why I'm making the choice I'm making. I might say, "I'm noticing that I've had enough. I want to keep having fun with you, but if I keep giving you piggyback rides, I will no longer be having fun. Can we find something else to do?" This response helps model for them the importance of listening to the body and the way they can use that information to set boundaries with others. It shows that my limit is a statement of care for myself and for them.

  - If a student asks if you will play with them, try responding with "Hm, I'm noticing my body is feeling heavy and tired. I don't have the capacity to play today. Can we play tomorrow if I'm feeling more energetic?" or "That question lit me up. I noticed the smile on my face as soon as you asked. I'd love to play." Speaking to how you pay attention to your body and use that information in your decision-making process will show them how they can do the same.

Coach It

- Create mini practice moments.

  - Throughout the day or the week, facilitate a body check like the one in step 3 of this lesson. Get students practiced in pausing, paying attention to their bodies, and using that information to make decisions that care for themselves and their needs.

- Cue your students to pause and pay attention to their bodies before responding.

  - As teachers, we're often in a rush, trying to fit everything we need to get done into the limited time we have. We might tell kids, "Decide already" or "Stop changing your mind." While a prompt to focus can be helpful for the student (and for the class), sometimes the situation calls for a moment of slowness rather than a push for speed.

  - When a student is struggling to make a decision, consider inviting them to pause, take a deep breath, and listen to what their body is saying. A deep breath helps the body and mind slow down. When we feel rushed by others (or by our own internal monologues), being still enough to pay attention to the body becomes a challenge. A reminder that it's okay to pause can go a long way. Use this reminder for yourself and for your students.

Boundary Statements

Learning Objectives:

By the end of this lesson, students will be able to:

1. Describe how awareness of their own boundaries and others' boundaries can help them make decisions.

2. Differentiate boundary statements from commands and opinions disguised as facts.

3. Create boundary statements.

Time: 40 minutes

Materials:

- Handout 4.2.1
- Scissors
- Tape or another method for hanging the statements from handout 4.2.1 on the board
- Worksheet 4.2.1
- Worksheet 4.2.2 (optional)
- Whiteboard
- Whiteboard markers

Before You Start:

- Read through the lesson plan.
- Print handout 4.2.1 and cut out each of the nine statements.
- Print worksheet 4.2.1 (one per student).
- Decide on which option in step 4 will best suit your class. If students will complete the worksheet on their own, print worksheet 4.2.2 (one per student).

Step 1   Introduce the Topic

Guide the class in taking two deep breaths.

Tell students that today you will be continuing to explore the topic of boundaries. Ask students what they remember about boundaries (from lesson 1.3).

After students respond, you can summarize: "A boundary separates two things from each other, much like a fence separates two yards. Today, we're going to be using boundaries to describe the difference between what is tolerable and what isn't tolerable, or what is comfortable and what is uncomfortable. What is tolerable or comfortable often changes based on how we're feeling, where we are, and who we're with."

Draw the following diagram on the board. Explain that when deciding on what to do with someone, thinking about the diagram can be helpful.

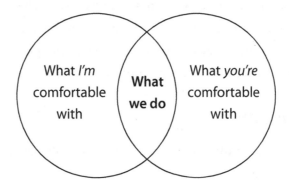

"When we practice consent, we navigate both people's limits (or boundaries) and both people's desires. We gather information about what we are comfortable with by noticing our bodies. We can gather information about what other people are comfortable with by talking to them and noticing their bodies too. Today, we're going to explore how to tell someone what we are not comfortable with—we're going to learn how to set boundaries."

Step 2 Activity + Discussion

Create a 4×4 table on the board. Label the columns and rows so that your table matches the one below:

Scenario	Command	Opinion Disguised as Fact	Boundary
A friend is yelling at you.			
A friend wants to play with you.			
A friend wants to hug you.			

On a separate area of the board, in a random order, hang up the nine pieces of paper from handout 4.2.1. Use a hanging method that allows you to easily move the pieces of paper around.

If relevant for your class, briefly define the terms *command* and *opinion disguised as fact*.

- A command is a statement in which one person tells another person what to do. For example: "Go do the laundry."

- An opinion disguised as fact is a statement in which one person says their opinion like it's an unarguable truth. For example: "Dogs are the best."

Explain how the activity works. Each of the nine pieces of paper contains a statement. The column on the left describes three scenarios. The labels on top describe what kind of statement it is. You will read aloud each of the nine statements and ask the students to tell you where they believe the statement belongs. Move the pieces of paper to their respective spaces on the board until the table is complete.

ANSWER KEY:

- **Command:** "Stop yelling." "You can only play with me for 10 minutes." "Don't hug me."

- **Opinion disguised as fact:** "Yelling is what crybabies do." "Playing with you is boring." "Hugs are dumb."

- **Boundary:** "Please don't yell at me. I am not okay with that." "I can play with you but only for 10 minutes." "I am not comfortable hugging you right now."

DISCUSSION QUESTIONS:

- What differences do you notice between the different kinds of statements (commands, opinions disguised as facts, and boundaries)?

  - *Talking points:* In all of these statements, we get a sense of what the person speaking wants and doesn't want. But boundary statements are special because the person uses the word *I*. Unlike telling the other person what to do, or sharing their opinion like absolute fact, a boundary usually involves sharing an "I" statement to let the other person know what we are or are not comfortable with. When setting boundaries, as much as possible, try to talk about what *you're* comfortable with, what *your* limits are, or what *you're* willing to do, rather than talking about what someone else *has* to do.

- Does this mean that it's wrong to say commands like "You can't yell at me" or "Don't hug me"?

  - *Talking points:* No. These lessons are not here to police language or tell students what they can and cannot do. A big take-home point from all of these lessons is that there are many ways to communicate and interact. Navigating a situation depends on the situation we're in, who we're with, the skills we have, the mental resources available to us, and so on. If someone is going in for a hug without asking or after we've shared a hug boundary, it might be a very good idea to say "Don't hug me." This activity is here to draw students' attention to how their communication might be received (and how they might receive another person's communication) so that they can make choices accordingly. If a student gets frustrated because their friend said "Don't hug me" when they asked for a hug, the friend might be able to recognize that their boundary was more of a command and they now have some language and tools for seeing that and beginning repair accordingly.

- Does this mean that it's wrong to say opinions disguised as facts, like "Playing with you is boring" or "Hugs are dumb"?

  - *Talking points:* These are slightly different kinds of statements. I can't think of a situation where it would be kind to either person to say "Playing with you is boring." It's never kind to be dismissive of another person by labeling them. It's also not kind to label foods or activities negatively. We don't want to yuck someone's yum. I can imagine a scenario where a student is sharing how frustrated they are that their grandma tries to tell them that they have to give her a hug. In that case, if they say "Hugs are dumb," it may be the time to remind them, "You mean that you don't like hugs," but it is totally reasonable to leave it and let them have their moment of venting. Trying to set a boundary by stating an opinion as fact is different from venting to a friend. I'm definitely guilty of saying "Dogs are the best" when admiring my pet. But if I wouldn't respond to a friend asking me if I wanted to pet their cat by saying that same statement.

Step 3   Activity + Discussion

Introduce worksheet 4.2.1 to the class and review the instructions. Give students about five minutes to complete the worksheet. Once students have completed it, review the answers together. (Keep in mind that students will learn the difference between assertive, aggressive, and submissive in lesson 4.3, and some questions might be answered there.)

DISCUSSION QUESTION:

- What's the difference between a preference and a boundary?

  - *Talking points:* A preference is more flexible than a boundary. A preference says, "Here's what I'd like to do/have, but I'm willing to adjust." A boundary says, "Here's my limit. This is what I'm comfortable with." When someone shares a preference, they might be okay with not getting what they want. For example, if a student says they want to play tag first and then play video games, they are sharing a preference. If a student says that they are only willing to play with a friend if they can play tag first (perhaps because they have energy they need to get out), they are sharing a boundary.

  - Boundaries aren't always inflexible. In the video game/tag scenario, the friend might suggest they play a different active game and then do video games, and that might be a solution that works for all. Boundaries aren't necessarily rigid, but they are less flexible than preferences.

  - Because boundaries convey a limit, if someone dismisses or crosses a boundary, there is a consequence. If a student tells the class about their friend's secret crush, their friend will probably trust them less. If a friend keeps canceling a playdate last-minute even though you told them this messes up your plans, you might no longer invite them over to play. These aren't punishments for crossing a boundary; these are natural consequences that come with not respecting another person's limits. Sometimes the potential consequences will be made clear before they unfold, but sometimes not.

Supporting This Lesson in Your Classroom's Culture

Model It

- Take notice when you're setting boundaries, making requests, giving commands, and sharing opinions disguised as facts.

  - When you can, use a boundary statement or a request. Instead of saying "That's gross" when a student picks their nose, you can say "Please get a tissue" or "I'll need you to wash your hands before we can move on." Instead of saying "Don't take my markers," you can say "Please ask me before borrowing my supplies" or "I'm not comfortable with you taking my belongings without asking first." We're not looking for a 100 percent success rate. You will still make commands and share opinions as if they are facts. The goal here is to model more precise and thoughtful communication and boundary setting.

Coach It

- Use language adjustments to support better boundary setting.

  ○ We're all guilty of sharing our opinions like they're facts. "That's awful" and "That's gorgeous" are both opinions! When a student is telling another student their idea is "dumb" or their way of playing isn't "right," rephrase the statement. "Your idea is dumb" turns into "I don't like that idea." "Your way of playing isn't right" turns into "I've never played that way." When you make corrections like this, you subtly demonstrate that you're not comfortable with this kind of communication in your classroom while modeling alternatives to help get them in the habit of using more "I" statements.

- Respect boundary setting directed at you.

  ○ When a student tells you they're not comfortable with something you're doing or did, take note. Thank them for giving you that information and share what you will do differently. Setting boundaries is challenging, especially when you're the person in the relationship with less power. When we accept students' boundaries and even thank them, we teach students how to receive a boundary when they have power. This is how we prepare them to hear a no with grace.

Handout 4.2.1

"Stop yelling."	"You can only play with me for 10 minutes."	"Don't hug me."
"Yelling is what crybabies do."	"Playing with you is boring."	"Hugs are dumb."
"Please don't yell at me. I am not okay with that."	"I can play with you but only for 10 minutes."	"I am not comfortable hugging you right now."

Worksheet 4.2.1

Directions: Review each statement pair. Circle the statement that best exemplifies a boundary. Decide which of the two statements best says, "This is what I am (or am not) comfortable with."

Hint: Look for statements with the words *I* or *my*. Consider which statement you'd prefer to hear from a friend.

1. People who litter are bad.   Please don't litter on my yard.

2. I won't play with you if you keep making fun of me.   Stop being mean.

3. You're not listening to me!   Please look at me while I am talking to you.

4. I don't want to play soccer today.   Soccer is boring.

5. You have to play with me.   I would like to play with you. How does checkers sound?

6. I'm not free now. I will come over once I finish my homework.   You should know that I'm not free.

Worksheet 4.2.2

Directions: Consider how you can respond with a boundary (or set a boundary) in each of these scenarios. Think about how you might feel and what you might want. Write the boundary statement in the blank space provided.

> **EXAMPLE:**
> **Scenario:** David is playing loud music, and it's bothering you.
> **Boundary:** *This music is too loud for me. Please turn it down.*

1. **Scenario:** Aunt Alondra tries to get you to eat a piece of pie, but you're not interested.

   Boundary:

3. **Scenario:** Shankar begs you to share your homework answers. You'd like him to stop.

   Boundary:

4. **Scenario:** Robin starts playing with your toys without asking. You'd like her to stop.

   Boundary:

5. **Scenario:** Chen poked you, and you didn't like it.

   Boundary:

6. **Scenario:** Conner wants you to play chess with him, but you don't want to play chess.

   Boundary:

Aggressive, Assertive, and Submissive

Learning Objectives:

By the end of this lesson, students will be able to:

1. Define *aggressive*, *assertive*, and *submissive*.

2. Identify how aggressiveness, assertiveness, and submissiveness sound in their own voices.

3. Demonstrate assertive communication.

4. Demonstrate compassion for themselves when they don't set an assertive boundary.

Time: 20 minutes

Materials:

- Script 4.3.1
- Worksheet 4.3.1 (optional)
- Whiteboard
- Whiteboard markers

Before You Start:

- Read through the lesson plan.
- Print script 4.3.1 (two copies).
- Decide on which option in step 3 will best suit your class. If students will complete the worksheet on their own, print worksheet 4.3.1 (one per student).

Step 1   Introduce the Topic

Guide the class in taking two deep breaths.

Tell students that in today's lesson, you will continue to explore how to set boundaries.

Ask students to raise their hand if they've ever felt unkind when setting a boundary or saying no.

Then say, "There are unkind ways to say no or set boundaries. However, in general, saying no isn't mean, rude, or unkind. What's the difference between setting a boundary in a kind way and in an unkind way?" Invite students to answer.

Write the words *aggressive*, *assertive*, and *submissive* on the board. Ask students if they are familiar with these words and invite them to explain what each means. You'll share the definitions in step 2.

"When a friend invites you to join in an activity or requests that you play with them, hug them, or sleep over at their house, and you want to say no, there are three ways you can respond: aggressively, assertively, or submissively. We're going to build off what you know and examine each."

Step 2   Skit + Discussion

Invite a student to volunteer to perform three very short scenarios with you. If no students are interested in volunteering, ask another teacher to play the student role. Hand them a copy of script 4.3.1.

Perform the three skits. Offer a round of applause for the volunteer and ask them to return to their seat.

Ask the class to label which skit demonstrated an aggressive response, an assertive response, and a submissive response. Then share the following definitions:

"When you are aggressive, it tells a person that you only care about your wants. Aggression can look like interrupting, sound like a loud voice, and feel like anger." Ask students if they have any other features of aggression to add.

"When you are assertive, it tells a person that you care about your wants and their wants. Assertiveness can look like taking turns to speak, sound like a calm yet firm voice, and feel like kind strength." Ask students if they have any other features of assertiveness to add.

"When you are submissive, it tells a person that you only care about their wants. Submission can look like not speaking up or like hesitating. It can feel like you have no other option but to do what the other person wants." Ask students if they have any other features of submissiveness to add.

"Sometimes our aggressive sides or submissive sides can be running the show, but as much as possible we want to be assertive when setting boundaries and when communicating in general."

Step 3   Activity

Introduce worksheet 4.3.1 to the class and review the instructions. With younger students, you might decide to do this activity as a class. If you choose the independent worksheet option, give students about five minutes to complete it. Once students are done, review the answers together.

Whichever option you choose, ask students what they notice about the features of each response. Refer back to the lesson on nonverbal cues and tone of voice (lesson 3.1).

You can point out:

- "I" language vs. "you" language: Assertive boundaries include "I" statements.

- The length of the responses: If the statement is very short, it likely doesn't acknowledge both people's perspectives.

- The emotion(s) you're picking up on: Assertive boundaries are shared calmly, without exclamation.

- Whether it involves collaboration or a command: Demands and commands aren't part of assertive boundary statements.

- Whether the person is sharing their no: Assertive boundaries tell the other person that what they have suggested, requested, or already done isn't something you're okay with.

Step 4   Discussion

DISCUSSION QUESTIONS:

- Is it ever okay to share a boundary more aggressively or without using an "I" statement?

  ○ *Talking points:* Definitely. If someone takes something of yours without asking or touches you in a way that you're not okay with, and you need them to stop what they're doing immediately, you might say, "Stop!" Once they've stopped, you can more calmly explain to them that you weren't okay with their actions. You can use assertive boundary guidelines to help you more calmly communicate what you're feeling and why you acted the way you did. You might also choose to share a boundary more aggressively once you've already shared an assertive boundary and they aren't respecting it. In moments like these, sharing a short firm statement like "I said no" might be an important step in keeping your limits safe. We'll talk more about this in a future lesson (lesson 5.1).

- When a person gives a not-so-sure yes or a yes that seems submissive, it can feel like they're saying yes even though they want to say no. Is it ever okay to say yes even when you're feeling like a no?

  - *Talking points:* Remember the difference between want to, willing to, and enduring. When you say yes even though you don't really *want* to say yes, consider if you are willing to or enduring. There are also times when you're feeling a no, but for your health and safety, you must say yes. Remind students about decisions that others need to be a part of. Last, you might say yes because you feel scared to say no. When this happens, the best thing to do is talk to a trusted adult so you can figure out how to handle the situation you were just in and what you can do if that situation arises again. We'll talk more about this in the coming lessons.

- Share a memory of a time when you said yes but wished you'd said no (e.g., going to a friend's birthday dinner when you weren't feeling well or joining a committee you didn't have time for). Share what that felt like, that it's okay you made that choice, and what you learned from that situation.

Supporting This Lesson in Your Classroom's Culture

Model It

- Rephrase your words and coach students in rephrasing their words.

  - When you notice your no is becoming more aggressive than assertive, call it out. Say out loud that you're noticing your style of speech is harsh and aggressive, and restate your no assertively. You can also call on students to help you rephrase. This is a great opportunity for them to practice finding an assertive way to say no while also helping them become more likely to get on board with your answer.

Coach It

- Pay attention to submissive yeses.

  - When you overhear a seemingly submissive yes, you can check in with the student by asking, "Is that a real willing yes, or are you trying to find the words to say no?" From here, you can either remind the student that it's okay to say no or you can coach them in collaborating so that the yes is more genuine.

- Pay attention to aggressive boundaries.

    ○ When you overhear aggressive speech from a student, you might coach them into using more assertive language. Before you do so, however, make sure that you have a clear sense of context. If this is a student's fourth time saying no, and their peer isn't respecting their no, it's not a time to focus on the aggressiveness of the boundary. That's a time to help the peer cope with the no.

    ○ If the student started from a place of aggression and you believe it's time to do some coaching, consider whether the student is regulated. If they're dysregulated, it's not a time for coaching. A student needs to be regulated and open enough to receive your feedback. Maybe you offer that they can come to a more private area to try a coping strategy, or maybe you suggest the other students provide some space. Use whatever strategy will be most helpful for maintaining trust and facilitating learning.

Script 4.3.1

SET THE SCENE: "Imagine you're at a friend's house and they want to play a specific video game."

Scenario 1:

TEACHER: Hey, let's play this adventure video game.

STUDENT: Uh, sure.

Scenario 2:

TEACHER: Hey, let's play this adventure video game.

STUDENT: You don't get to choose. I'm the guest, I decide what video game we play.

Scenario 3:

TEACHER: Hey, let's play this adventure video game.

STUDENT: I don't like that game. How do you feel about playing that car-racing game instead? Or maybe the dragon one you showed me last time?

Worksheet 4.3.1

Directions: Review each statement. In the boxes to the right, give examples of ways a person can respond to each statement by being aggressive, assertive, or submissive.

When a Person Says . . .	Aggressive Response	Assertive Response	Submissive Response
Give me some of your snack.	You can't tell me what to do!	I'm not finished with my snack yet. If I have some left over when I'm finished, I can give you that.	Okay, take whatever you want.
I want to wrestle with you.			
Give me a hug.			

Minds Change

Learning Objectives:

By the end of this lesson, students will be able to:

1. Identify three reasons why a person would change their response from a yes to a no.

2. Demonstrate how to change their yes to a no.

3. Describe the factors to consider in balancing commitment with the freedom to change one's mind.

4. Demonstrate compassion for themselves when they change from a yes to a no.

5. Describe the purpose and importance of checking in.

Time: 45 minutes

Materials:

- Worksheet 4.4.1
- Whiteboard
- Whiteboard markers

Before You Start:

- Read through the lesson plan.
- Decide on a personal anecdote to share in step 3.
- Print worksheet 4.4.1 (one per student).
- Decide how you will pair up students in step 4.

Step 1   Introduce the Topic

Guide the class in taking two deep breaths.

"We've spent the last few lessons talking about the experience of setting boundaries or saying no when you're figuring out what to do (or not do) with someone. But after you've made a plan, and even after your plan is underway, you are still allowed to say no (or say stop) and set new boundaries. Our minds change all the time, and we honor ourselves and our limits by noticing these changes and speaking up accordingly.

"When a person switches from a yes to a no, they might say that they *changed their mind*. But this expression misses what's really happening. A person doesn't choose to change their mind in the same way that they might choose to change their clothes or the game they're playing. When someone says 'I changed my mind,' what they're actually saying is 'I'm *noticing* something in my mind, my thoughts, my emotions, and my body—and now that I have this information, it's important for me to change my answer.' When a friend says 'I've changed my mind,' it can sound like they've *decided* to feel or think differently, when really, it's more likely that they've noticed something new and are speaking up so that they don't cross their own limits and feel uncomfortable with their decision.

"Today, we're going to explore why a person might switch from a yes to a no and get some practice in navigating situations where we *notice* a change in heart or mind."

Step 2 Discussion

Tell students that you're going to look at three scenarios. Share each of the scenarios, followed by their respective discussion questions:

Scenario 1:

"It's cake time at Lola's best friend's birthday party. Her friend's mom brings out a yellow cake with white frosting. Vanilla is Lola's favorite! She's so excited to dig in, but when she takes her first bite, she realizes it's not vanilla flavored, it's lemon. Lola doesn't like lemon cake, so she finds a napkin, gently spits out the cake, drinks some water, and continues hanging out with her friends."

DISCUSSION QUESTION:

- Why did Lola change from a yes to a no in this scenario?
  - *Talking points:* The experience wasn't what she thought it would be.

Scenario 2:

"It's cake time at Lola's best friend's birthday party. Her friend's mom brings out a yellow cake with white frosting. It's Lola's favorite! She asks for a big piece, but halfway through, she realizes her eyes were bigger than her stomach and she's too full to finish the whole piece. Lola sets it aside and lets her stomach digest as she continues talking to her friends and enjoying the party."

DISCUSSION QUESTION:

- Why did Lola change from a yes to a no in this scenario?

    ○ *Talking points:* She'd had enough. She enjoyed it but then didn't want any more.

Scenario 3:

"It's cake time at Lola's best friend's birthday party. Her friend's mom brings out a yellow cake with white frosting. It's Lola's favorite, but she's full from the pizza they served earlier. Even though she doesn't want a slice, she decides to accept one because that's what everyone else is doing. As she lifts up her fork to take her first bite, Lola remembers that she doesn't have to eat cake just because everyone else is eating cake. She puts her fork down and offers her slice to a friend who didn't get one yet."

DISCUSSION QUESTION:

- Why did Lola change from a yes to a no in this scenario?

    ○ *Talking points:* She realized she'd said yes even though she was feeling like a no. She wasn't a yes at all, and if she ate the cake, she would be enduring.

Conclude the conversation: "Sometimes you say yes, possibly even an enthusiastic yes, but then, for one reason or another, you start to notice you're a no. It's okay to change your response. You can always say no or stop—and if you hear a no or stop from someone else, you need to respect that too."

Step 3 Activity

Share your own experience of a time when you changed your response from a yes to a no. Try to find an example that goes deeper than the example scenarios. Share the reasons for your changed response, how you felt after making the decision, how others reacted, and how you felt about their reactions. Then introduce worksheet 4.4.1 to the class and review the instructions.

Give students about five minutes to complete the worksheet. When students are done, invite some students to share their responses. Point out the variety of reasons why students changed from a yes to a no and what the reactions from others around them were. Briefly refer back to lesson 3.3 and the conversations you had about how to receive a boundary or a no.

Wrap up the activity by reinforcing that it's totally common and okay to have a change of mind and to then change your response. Even though it might be hard to hear that someone's willingness has changed, it's important to respect their choice.

Step 4   Activity

In this activity, students will pair up to practice changing their responses from yes to no. In each pair, one student will start as student A and one as student B before switching roles.

Explain to students that they're going to practice changing their responses from yes to no.

"Student A will suggest a game or movement activity. Student B will say yes or collaborate until both students are genuinely comfortable with the game plan. Then you'll both start the activity. About 30 seconds into the activity, student B will tell student A that they've noticed a change of mind and want to stop or change something about what they're doing. Student A will respond kindly.

"Here's an example of what this might look like: If my partner and I decide to do 60 jumping jacks, at some point before we're done, I'm going to stop and tell them I'm noticing I'm too tired for this, or maybe I'll tell them that it feels funny to jump while facing them, so I'm going to keep going but while facing the wall."

As with the collaboration practice in lesson 3.5, students can pick from options like stretching, doing jumping jacks, doing a staring contest, playing charades, playing Pictionary, and so forth. Remind students that the activity they pick needs to be one that won't disrupt other students.

After the first round is complete, do the practice again with student B in the initiating role and student A in the changing-mind role.

When students are done, invite them back to their seats and discuss the experience as a group.

DISCUSSION QUESTIONS:

- What was that experience like?

  - *Talking points:* There's no right answer. Discuss what the experience was like for them.

- What emotions did you feel when it came time **to tell your partner** you wanted to stop or change something? Did you notice any feelings in your body?

  - *Talking points:* Students might share that they felt "bad." See if you can get them to expand on that feeling. Did they feel like they were being mean?

Doing something wrong? Guilty for changing their response and "ruining" the fun? They might have observed that it was hard to speak up or that it felt like they had a pit in their stomach. There's no right way to feel. Any observation they have is valid.

- What emotions did you feel when **your partner told you** they wanted to stop or wanted a change? Did you notice any feelings in your body?

    ○ *Talking points:* Students might share that they felt "bad." See if you can get them to expand on that feeling. Did they feel like they were being accused of doing something wrong? Did they feel guilty about the possibility that they made a mistake and this is why the person told them to stop? They might have observed tightness in the muscles or their cheeks getting warm. There's no right way to feel. Any observation they have is valid.

- Is there anything you might do differently next time?

    ○ *Talking points:* Would they have chosen different words? Changed their tone or body language? Why would they make these choices if they were to do this exercise again?

- Would it be okay for the person who made the original request to change their response from a yes to a no? For example, if I ask you to do a puzzle with me, is it okay for me to decide halfway through that I want to stop?

    ○ *Talking points:* Yes. All people's boundaries matter, regardless of when those boundaries come up or whose they are.

- We talked about changing from a yes to a no, but is it okay for someone to change from a no to a yes?

    ○ *Talking points:* Yes! This comes up a lot in new experiences. You might say no at first and then see someone else try it and what it looks like and decide you're a yes.

- Is it possible for someone to take advantage of changing their response? Maybe often saying yes and then deciding last-minute they're a no? Or maybe changing their mind so often that it feels like you never know where they're at?

    ○ *Talking points:* This is a tricky question where the concepts of willing, enduring, collaboration, and commitment come in handy. How can we balance the value of noticing our desires and our limits with the value of commitment (sticking to doing what we say we're going to do)?

Imagine that on Monday, someone invites you to have a sleepover on Saturday. At the time, you're really excited and you say yes. When Saturday rolls around, though, you notice your willingness has changed. Your feelings have shifted from "really excited" to "willing but not excited." Or maybe they've shifted from "really excited" to "enduring." These are important distinctions. What changed? Did you learn new information? Are you noticing you're not feeling well?

If you would be enduring, that's a sign to change your response. But it might also be an opportunity to collaborate on a new solution where you can show that you value both commitment and your limits. For example, you might suggest that you do a movie night but sleep at your own houses or offer them a sleepover at your house if that would be more comfortable. There's no right answer. It's about keeping in mind both your desires and limits *and* the other person's desires and limits. What would going to the sleepover mean for you? *And* what would not going mean for them?

Step 5 Discussion

"It can be difficult to tell someone you're changing your response from a yes to a no or that you need a change. In our lesson about being a better asker (lesson 2.3), we talked about ways you can make it easier for someone to give an honest answer before you make a request. But there is also something you can do to make it easier for someone to share their honest feelings *during* an interaction."

Ask the class how they can make it easier for someone to change their response or say stop during an interaction if they're noticing that something doesn't feel good.

Affirm any helpful answers that students provide, and then introduce the concept of checking in.

"To check in means to touch base or reconnect about something. You can check in during a relationship or during an interaction. Either way, the purpose of a check-in is to talk about how the experience or the relationship is going for each person. A check-in can sound like 'How is this feeling for you?' or 'Are you having fun?' or 'I want to change this. Is there anything you want to change?'

"Even our school knows that check-ins are important. It's why I have conferences with your parents and guardians during the school year. These conferences are a kind of check-in. I share how my experience has been and what I might need from them, as your adults. They share with me what their experience has been like and what they might need from me, as your teacher. If there's something urgent to address, we can also check in outside of these times.

"It's easier to share what's going on when someone asks you. It's harder to share what's going on when you have to do it all on your own. That's why checking in is so helpful. It invites the other person to share their feelings, which is a powerful way to show them that you care about *their* desires and boundaries—not just your own."

Ask students if they can think of times when it might be an especially good idea for them to check in with someone during an interaction.

Generate a list on the board. Answers might include:

- When you notice body cues that indicate they might not be enjoying themselves

- When you chose the activity

- When you've been doing the activity for a while

- When you feel like their yes might not reflect how they really feel

- When you notice they're not participating actively or the way that they're participating has shifted

"In this lesson, we've talked about how we can care for and respect our own desires and boundaries by sharing how we feel. And we can also care for and respect someone else's desires and boundaries by checking in with them to see if there's anything they want or need."

Supporting This Lesson in Your Classroom's Culture

Model It

- Create "teacher-student conferences."

  - Create a practice of checking in with students about how they're feeling about their learning, the classroom rules, their friendships. These should be separate from more formal academic check-ins and instead focused on their feelings about these areas of their school life.

- Reinforce a student's choice to change their mind with others (and with you).

  - Changing from a yes to a no can be challenging. Praising a student for doing this can help reaffirm them in this hard decision. This is especially important when others around them are showing frustration with their decision.

  - If a student is constantly changing their response, you can support them in making a decision by suggesting they take a breath and pause. If that doesn't help, you can ask if there's any missing information they need. If they are still struggling to make a choice, you can negotiate a decision together. For example, "You're having a hard time deciding. I want you to make a choice that feels good. We also need to move on as a class. I'd like you to take one more minute to decide, and then if you don't decide, I'll pick something for you to stick with. Can we do that?" You can also pick something for them and ask if they are willing to be a yes to that.

Coach It

- Remember that "But they said yes . . ." isn't a forever promise.

  - Refer back to lesson 3.2. A yes can become a no for all of the reasons discussed in this lesson.

  - Coach students to check in about their decisions. This can be done as a whole-group reminder. For example, during recess, you can make an announcement to remind students all at once to check in with the people they are playing with. You can do the same with group project time.

  - This can also be done on a one-to-one basis when you notice body language from a student that indicates they might not be on board with the activity.

Worksheet 4.4.1

Directions: It's okay to change your response from a yes to a no. Share your experience with changing your response in the spaces provided.

1. Describe a time when you said yes at first, but then shifted to a no or made an adjustment to your yes once you got started. (Try to share a story that's not about food.)

2. Why did you change your decision?

3. How did you feel about your decision?

4. How did the people around you react to your decision?

5. How did their reaction make you feel?

Because of What They're Doing (or Saying), Saying No Is Hard

Time:
45 minutes

Learning Objectives:

By the end of this lesson, students will be able to:

1. Describe the reasons why saying no can be challenging.

2. Demonstrate awareness of how their words and actions can put pressure on others.

3. Identify tactics that are used to create pressure.

4. Spot coercive language and correct it.

Materials:

- Worksheet 4.5.1
- Worksheet 4.5.2
- Whiteboard
- Whiteboard markers

Before You Start:

- Read through the lesson plan.
- Print worksheet 4.5.1 (one per student).
- Decide which option in step 4 best suits your class. If students will complete the worksheet on their own, print worksheet 4.5.2 (one per student).

Step 1   Introduce the Topic

Guide the class in taking two deep breaths.

"We've talked a lot about saying no, but saying no is one of those things that's often a lot easier said than done."

With students, generate a list of reasons why saying no can be hard or times when saying no can be hard. Based on their answers, generate a list on a flip chart so that you can easily refer back to this list in future lessons.

The list may include answers like:

- They're pressuring you.

- They have power or authority.

- You feel like you owe them.

- You fear that saying no will be uncomfortable.

- You believe it's rude to say no.

- You don't want to disappoint them.

- You feel like that's what they're expecting.

- You fear what will happen if you don't "go with the flow."

- You fear they won't respect your no anyway.

- You want to make them happy.

- You're not used to saying no.

- You fear what they will do to you if you say no.

Bring students' attention to all the reasons that saying no can be hard.

"Sometimes a friend's or adult's words or actions can make saying no a challenge. Sometimes our own beliefs or feelings, or even the little voice in our head, can make it hard to say no. In fact, saying no can be so hard that you might say (or you might hear someone say), 'I couldn't say no.' Saying no can be so challenging sometimes that it feels like we don't even have a choice, even though we should have a choice!

"Over the next few lessons, we're going to explore what makes saying no hard and what we can do in these moments. We're going to start by talking about how someone's actions or words can make saying no hard."

Step 2 Discussion

Ask the class if they're familiar with the term *peer pressure* and invite students to share what this concept means to them. If you've talked about peer pressure before, refer back to those conversations. Simply put, peer pressure is the experience of having peers, classmates, or friends try to influence your behaviors or decisions.

"Peer pressure is a powerful force. If a friend or a group of friends is telling you to say yes to something, you're going to feel pressured to say yes. Peer pressure isn't the only kind of type of pressure that can influence us, though. There are many ways we can be pushed to do something we don't want to do and many ways we might (accidentally or on purpose) push others to do something they don't want to do.

"There are a lot of words we can use to talk about this kind of pressure. *Manipulation, influence, control, coercion,* and *persuasion* are all words that refer to pushing someone's decision or behavior in a certain direction. While these words all have slightly different meanings, they are similar in that they are all tactics (or strategies) that can be used to weaken someone else's boundaries. From everything we've been discussing, we know that *both* people matter in an interaction. That means it's not okay for you to weaken or ignore someone else's boundaries, and it's not okay for someone else to weaken or ignore your boundaries."

Step 3   Activity + Discussion

Introduce worksheet 4.5.1 to the class and review the instructions. Give students about five minutes to complete the worksheet. Some of these ideas might be new to students. You can ask them to take a best guess. The purpose of this activity is to introduce students to the different ways we can intentionally or unintentionally take advantage of someone. It's not important for students to perfectly understand the terminology and definitions.

Once students have completed the worksheet, review the answers together.

ANSWER KEY: 1. Empty promises, 2. Bribing, 3. False logic, 4. Guilting, 5. Threatening social harm, 6. Creating doubts, 7. Threatening physical harm, 8. Repeating the request, 9. Physical intimidation

When you've finished reviewing the worksheet, ask, "By a show of hands, who's ever had a friend or sibling use one of these tactics on them?"

Then ask, "By a show of hands, who's ever used one of these tactics on a friend or sibling to get what they want?"

DISCUSSION QUESTIONS:

• How have statements like these and tactics like these made you feel? How do you think might they make someone else feel?

  ◦ *Talking points:* These tactics can make people scared to share their honest feelings and give genuine responses. They can make people feel like their boundaries and desires don't matter.

- These tactics can make us feel scared. How does fear show up in the body? What do you notice in your body when you're scared?

  ○ *Talking points:* Refer to discussions about body language in lesson 3.1 and discussions about body sensations in lesson 4.1.

- Is it possible for someone to use one of these tactics without recognizing what they are doing?

  ○ *Talking points:* Yes. Sometimes we get so focused on what we want, we lose track of how we might be making someone else feel. This is why we practice all of these skills: so that we can build our consent muscles and get better at navigating our desires and limits alongside others' desires and limits.

- What can you do if someone you have a healthy relationship with is using one of these pressure tactics on you?

  ○ *Talking points:* Point out to them that you're feeling pressured, let them know that your decision isn't changing, and so on. (We're going to be diving into this topic deeply in lesson 5.1, so gather a few responses and then let students know that there's more to come.)

Step 4 Activity

"It's totally okay to want things. It's even great because when you know what you want, you can ask for what you want. However, it's not okay to prioritize your wants over others' boundaries and say things that will make others feel pressured. Now that we know what *not* to say, let's explore what we *can* say in these moments instead."

Introduce worksheet 4.5.2 to the class and review the instructions. (For younger students, this activity might go more smoothly if you do it together on the board.) Give students about eight minutes to complete the worksheet. Once students have completed it, review their answers together.

Whichever option you go with, discuss new responses together as a class. Ask students what they notice about the adjusted responses. Point out the benefits of using "I" statements, sharing one's desires/feelings, and making requests.

Conclude the lesson by sharing that next time, you'll continue to talk about why saying no can be hard, and later on, you'll review what to do when someone is pressuring you.

Model It

- Consider how you might be using some of the pressuring tactics discussed. Reflect on what kind of influence or pressure is okay.

  - Parents and teachers often ask if it's ever okay to try to persuade a child. Where is the line between persuasion that's okay and persuasion that falls into coercion territory? The truth is, we are always persuading and influencing people. Because our brains react and change in response to outside stimuli, we are constantly being influenced or persuaded by the world around us. It's impossible to exist without persuading or being persuaded. When you smell freshly baked cookies, you may be persuaded to eat some baked goodies. When you hear a funny joke, you may be influenced to laugh. In fact, a comedian or friend might intentionally share a joke to evoke that specific response in you. Your romantic partner might try to conjure a certain feeling in you by putting on their favorite perfume or cologne. An activist might deliberately try to persuade you to speak up the next time you encounter hateful speech. I fully acknowledge that in writing this curriculum, I am trying to persuade you! Specifically, I'm trying to persuade you to take certain actions in your classrooms and with your students.

  - So when are influence and persuasion okay? I can't draw that line for you. That line is going to be different for different people in different situations. I can, however, provide you with a rule of thumb that I find helpful in answering this question: (1) If you aren't using coercive tactics and (2) you can say, out loud, how you're trying to influence them, you're likely okay. Here are two examples to demonstrate this idea:

    - In the introduction, when I told you this book is research-informed, I did so because it's true and because I hope it does some work in persuading you to implement this curriculum. I feel comfortable saying that out loud. I don't feel comfortable saying "This book will solve entitlement culture" in order to persuade you to implement the curriculum because that's a false promise. (Don't get me wrong, I think this book can have a huge positive impact, but I cannot honestly tell you that it will change our established culture.) I would feel uncomfortable saying that false promise out loud, so that's my cue that marketing this book with that slogan isn't an okay form of influence or persuasion. It tells me that I need to find a new strategy.

– Here's a classroom-related example: When you ask your student if they want to use a pen or pencil to complete their worksheet, you're giving them a choice about which writing instrument to use but not giving them choice on whether or not to do the assignment. Do you feel comfortable telling them that the reason you asked the question like that is because you want them to get the worksheet done and you're trying to help them find a way to do it that feels okay enough for them? If yes, then that's an okay influence in my mind! Meanwhile, if you tell a student "I'll be so sad if you don't do your assignment," you're most likely trying to guilt them into completing the assignment, which is a very different approach. Since you wouldn't say "I'm trying to guilt you into doing the assignment" out loud, that means you probably shouldn't tell a student "I'll be so sad if you don't do your assignment."

• If you feel tempted to say something that might fall into territory where you're putting undue pressure on a student, ask a clarifying question, make an observation, or share a request instead.

   ◦ Instead of telling a student "You're overreacting about the schedule," you can say "I'd like to know why you're feeling so strongly about the schedule today." Or you can observe, "Your voice got louder when you said you wouldn't go to lunch before recess. Can you tell me what's going on?"

   ◦ Instead of telling a student "If you don't do your homework, I'm going to take away your recess," try asking, "I need you to finish your homework. How can we make that happen?" You might also ask, "Are you willing to spend 10 minutes a night working on homework? For now, as long as you really work on it for 10 minutes, we can be all set." (You can put this in place as you work on whatever the bigger problem is around getting homework done.)

Coach It

• Resist the urge to label students' behavior as "coercive."

   ◦ The slogan "Coercion is not consent" has become popular across sexual violence awareness campaigns. As a result, I've noticed some teachers and parents inclined to label the behaviors of their students and kids as "coercive." While their intention, I imagine, is to help kids distinguish between behavior that is okay and not okay, there's a heaviness in the word *coercion* that might not suit the situation, and there's a lot lost in using a simple label.

- Instead of telling a student "You're pressuring them" or "That's coercion," prompt them to look inward and use their problem-solving skills. You can ask them to consider whether they already got an answer, to think about if anything they're doing might make it hard for their friend to give an honest answer, or to rewind and double-check whether there's a kinder way to say what they want to say. You can also tell the student "I'd feel guilty about saying no if you said that to me" or "Can you really promise them they're going to love it?"

- These alternatives bring focus to the words and actions they're choosing, to the impact those words and actions have on others, and to ways they can shift their language or actions to make the other person feel more comfortable sharing their real feelings.

Worksheet 4.5.1

There are a number of ways that someone might use pressure or influence to control your decisions and behaviors. This means that there are also a number of ways that you might, by accident or on purpose, use pressure or influence to control someone else's decisions and behaviors. Let's examine these kinds of pressure so we can identify them and know what to do if we see these behaviors in ourselves or in others.

Directions: Using the word bank, write down the pressure tactic or strategy that you believe best matches each description.

Guilting	Repeating the request	Empty promises
Threatening physical harm	Bribing	Creating doubts
Threatening social harm	Physical intimidation	False logic

1. Promising an outcome that you can't guarantee or don't have control over.

   Example: *"If you do this, you'll love it"* or *"Just do it. You're going to have so much fun."*

2. Promising a favor or gift to someone in order to influence their decision or behavior.

   Example: *"If you _____, I'll tell everyone that you have the most fun house to hang out at"* or *"If you _____, I'll give you five dollars."*

3. Using reasoning that is weak or not supported to convince someone to say yes.

Example: *"We should be doing this already because we've been dating for three months"* or *"I did this for you, so you have to do it for me."*

4. Making someone feel ashamed, responsible, or at fault because of the decision they want to make.

Example: *"Aww, I'll be so sad if you don't _____"* or *"A good friend would say yes."*

5. Threatening to damage the person's reputation if you don't get what you want.

Example: *"If you don't _____, I'm going to stop inviting you to my parties"* or *"If you don't do this, I'm going to tell everyone that you _____."*

6. Making someone question their reality so they start to doubt their reasoning for saying no.

Example: *"You're overreacting," "You don't actually feel that way,"* or *"You're not making sense, trust me."*

7. Threatening to inflict pain or injury to the person's body if you don't get what you want.

   Example: *"If you don't do it, I'll punch you."*

8. Repeating a request that's already been answered.

   Example: *"C'mon, please" or "Please, please, please."*

9. Using your body's distance from another person or your body language to get someone to agree with you or do what you want them to do.

   Example: *Getting really close to another person while standing face-to-face or clenching your fists like you are preparing to hit them.*

Worksheet 4.5.2

Directions: Read each statement. Create a new statement (or question) that will allow the other person to respond more honestly.

Hint: If someone were talking to you, how might they say what they want to say in a way that is kinder to you and your perspective?

EXAMPLE:

Instead of saying: *Just do this cheer move with me. You're going to have so much fun.*

I can say: *This cheer move is so fun for me. I think you might have fun doing it too. Would you be willing to give it a try?*

Or: *Will you please try this cheer move with me? I think it's one of the most fun ones out there.*

---

1. **Instead of saying:** *I gave you a massage, so you have to give me one.*

   I can say:

2. **Instead of saying:** *I'll be so sad if you don't hang out with me.*

   I can say:

3. **Instead of saying:** *If you don't tell me, I'm going to stop inviting you to my parties.*

   I can say:

4. **Instead of saying:** *You're overreacting. Sleeping in the same bed isn't a big deal.*

> **I can say:**

5. **Instead of saying:** *C'mon, please, please, please give me a piggyback ride.*

> **I can say:**

Because of What I Believe, Saying No Is Hard

Learning Objectives:

By the end of this lesson, students will be able to:

1. Describe how a person's beliefs can make it harder for them to say no.

2. Reflect on their beliefs about saying no.

3. Demonstrate how to say no when they feel like they owe someone a yes.

4. Identify strategies they can use when their beliefs are getting in the way of their ability to share their boundaries.

Time: 45 minutes

Materials:

- The flip chart you created in lesson 4.5
- Worksheet 4.6.1
- Worksheet 4.6.2
- Small candies

Before You Start:

- Read through the lesson plan.
- Decide which option in step 2 best suits your class. If students will complete the worksheet on their own, print worksheet 4.6.1 (one per student).
- Print worksheet 4.6.2 (one per student).
- Decide how you will pair up students in step 4.
- Purchase small candies (one per student).

Step 1 — Introduce the Topic

Hang up the flip chart you created in lesson 4.5 at the front of the classroom.

Guide the class in taking two deep breaths.

"Last time, we spoke about how the things another person does or says can make it hard for someone to say no. Today, we're going to explore how someone's *beliefs* can make it hard for them to say no."

Step 2   Activity

"By a show of hands, who has ever been told to 'just say no'?"

After students respond, say, "Even though saying no can be so hard, people give this advice all the time. But it's a myth that saying no is easy or something we can 'just do.'" (If relevant for your class, introduce or review the term *myth* with students.)

Introduce worksheet 4.6.1 to the class and review the instructions. Give students about three minutes to complete it. (For younger students, you may decide to do this activity together as a class.)

Once students have completed the worksheet, review the answers by asking students to show a thumbs-up for "true" and a thumbs-down for "false." Check to see if there are any questions along the way. As you review the responses, discuss how beliefs about the right ways to act can influence how we feel about saying yes or no. Sometimes these beliefs are so strong that it feels like we don't even have a choice (e.g., When someone is sad, we might feel like we have to say yes, or when someone gives us a gift and then asks for a hug, we might feel like we have to say yes).

ANSWER KEY:

1. **False.** Saying no isn't rude. An aggressive no isn't kind, but it's the aggression that makes it that way—not the no. Telling someone an assertive no to playing a game, to affection, or to doing something that doesn't feel good in your body is always okay!

2. **True.** Being honest and respectful about boundaries is what keeps relationships healthy and strong. We can only be our true selves if we are free to share both our likes and our dislikes, and if we have our likes and dislikes respected.

3. **True.** When you ask someone for permission *before* you engage in an action (like giving them a kiss on the cheek), you make it a safer space for them to give their honest response.

4. **False.** There are many ways to thank someone for their kindness. You can use words, write a note, give a hug (if they want one), or give a gift. While it's kind to at least say thank you, you never owe anyone any specific kind of response.

5. **False.** You're not responsible for how someone else receives your response. If someone gets upset or embarrassed by your assertive no, those are their feelings to navigate. You do not need to change your answer. Their feelings of disappointment or sadness are not more important than your right to your limits.

6. **False.** If it makes someone feel bad or uncomfortable, it's not a joke. "It was just a joke" is not an excuse to cross someone's boundaries.

Step 3   Activity

Introduce worksheet 4.6.2 to the class and review the instructions. Share a belief and story of your own to model what this looks like. Give students about eight minutes to complete the worksheet. If students are struggling to come up with experiences, try asking them to replace "I believe" with "I feel like."

Once students have completed the worksheet, ask them to share if they would like to. As they share, refer back to some of the items on the flip chart list to reinforce that these are common experiences.

The next lesson will explore how a person's position can make it harder for them to say no. If students ask about saying no to teachers, to authority, or to older siblings, you can let them know you'll be talking more about these situations next time.

Step 4   Practice

In this activity, students will pair up to practice saying no. In each pair, one student will start as student A and one as student B before switching roles. Explain to students that they're going to practice saying no.

In round 1, instruct students to enact the following script:

Student A: "Can I have a hug?"

Student B: "No."

Student A: "Okay." (or some other kind-enough response)

Then have students switch roles. When both partners have had a turn, facilitate a short debrief. Ask students how it felt to say no. There are no right answers.

If students ask if they can say yes, let them know that you're glad they want to say yes, but to get practice in saying no, the instructions are to say no.

In round 2, give each student a piece of candy and instruct them to do as follows:

Student B: *gives student A a piece of candy*

Student B: "Can I have a hug?"

Student A: "No."

Then have students switch roles. When both partners have had a turn, facilitate a short debrief. Ask students how it felt to say no after their friend gave them a gift (the candy). There are no right answers.

For additional practice, you can facilitate a round where one student gives the other a compliment before asking for a hug.

To conclude this exercise, ask students if doing this brought up any memories, thoughts, or feelings that they'd like to share. Remind students not to name names.

Note: If a student insists that saying no is easy, explore it instead of fighting it. Here are some options for handling a moment like this:

- You can reinforce that it's a great feeling when we can say no with ease and protect our limits. It looks like they have some good saying-no skills in their toolbelt. And like with all skills, it's important to practice.

- You can accept their stance with a slight adjustment: "It sounds like saying no comes easily to you. That doesn't mean it comes easily to others." It's okay if they're not on board at first mention of this. You can talk about when saying no is harder and easier. Hard and easy aren't two distinct categories. Have them rate situations if that would feel more aligned for them. Do what you can to encourage them to listen and explore.

- Support them by helping them *feel* that saying no is hard.

  - One of my boldest teaching moments took place in an eighth-grade classroom. It was in the second of three sessions I led in their classroom. I introduced the idea that saying no is hard and got pushback from a student. They insisted that saying no is easy. After some back-and-forth, I walked over to the student's desk, picked up their backpack from the floor and walked it back to the teacher's desk. Every student in the classroom turned their heads to see one another's reactions. I asked the class, "Was what I did okay?" The students all said no. I replied, "Why didn't you say no, then?" The student conceded.

  - This strategy isn't a recommendation. It felt right in this moment with this student and class. However, I do recommend that you find a way to help that student feel like saying no is hard. This can be in the moment or by conversation where they reflect on times saying no has been hard. You can reference a TV show or movie they've seen where a character struggles to say no. Use what you know about that student.

Step 5   Discussion

DISCUSSION QUESTIONS:

- How does it feel to have a thought like "They gave me a gift, so I have to say yes" or "They're going to be disappointed if I don't say yes, so I should say yes"?

  - *Talking points:* Discuss how our own thoughts can put pressure on us. The beliefs we have about saying no (discussed in worksheet 4.6.2) can become little voices in our head that tell us we *must* say yes. This is a common experience. It can lead us to experience feelings of dread, fear, and being trapped.

- What do you notice in your body in response to these thoughts?

  - *Talking points:* Some common experiences might include the feeling of your heart racing, a pit in your stomach, sweating, and restlessness or jitteriness. If students are struggling to respond, have them consider a time when they had one of these thoughts (they can refer to their responses to worksheet 4.6.2). Ask them what they remember their bodies feeling like at that time. Often, our own thoughts can pressure us in the same way that other people's words do.

- What can you do when you notice these body sensations in response to your thoughts?

  - *Talking points:* Calm the nervous system by practicing deep breathing, counting to 10, repeating self-affirmations that it's okay to say no, or using other coping tools. From there, you can ask for some time to make a decision or consider collaborating so you aren't saying yes or saying no.

OPTIONAL DISCUSSION:

- Ask students where these beliefs about saying yes and saying no come from. Ask them to suggest how we can do our part to counteract these beliefs. You can write their answers on the board or on a flip chart.

  - *Talking points:* These messages come from media, family, friends, culture, religion, and so on. We can counteract these beliefs by paying attention to them, naming them, and recognizing that having a thought doesn't mean that the thought is true. Just because I think saying no is rude doesn't mean it is rude. We can also remind each other that it's okay to say no. It's important for each of us to honor our limits and each other's limits (whether those limits have been stated or not).

Supporting This Lesson in Your Classroom's Culture

Model It

- Consider how and when you use the word *just*.

  - There's an assumption of ease implied in the word *just*. But often the things being asked of us aren't easy. "Just say no" is a prime example of this. Consider where in your everyday teaching and conversations you use the idea of "just say no" or "just ask." If a student is having trouble saying no, you can empathize with them, strategize with them, and practice with them instead.

Coach It

- Myth-bust when you can.

  - When you hear one student talking to another about how they "have to" say yes, refer back to this lesson. Remind students that it's easy to believe that we're supposed to say yes or that others are supposed to say yes in certain moments. But, in truth, we should only say yes if it would feel okay to do so. Say yes if you *want* to say yes. You can also say yes if you're *genuinely willing* to say yes. However, you never *have* to say yes to touch, a game, a playdate, and so on. You have choice! The only time you might have to say yes, or might not have choice, is for health and safety reasons. Remind students about this regularly.

- When they say "You're making me," remind them that you're not.

  - When a student says "You're making me do this worksheet" or "You're forcing me to sit next to them," remind them that this isn't so. They have choice. There are consequences to those choices, but they still have choice. You cannot force them to do anything. Likely, what's actually happening is that you are sharing information with them about what your expectations are, how their behavior impacts the class or another student, or what other consequences their choices have. What they do is up to them. You're there to support them in making decisions that they will feel good about.

Worksheet 4.6.1

This is a myth-busting activity. We're going to explore some truths and untruths about saying no.

Directions: Indicate whether you believe each statement is true (T) or false (F).

_____ **1.** Saying no is rude.

_____ **2.** Strong relationships are built on respect for each other's boundaries.

_____ **3.** Saying no to "Do you want a kiss on the cheek?" is easier than saying stop to someone already kissing you on the cheek.

_____ **4.** If someone is kind to you, hosts you, or gives you a gift, you owe them the kind of thank-you that they want.

_____ **5.** If someone feels bad because you said no, you should change your answer.

_____ **6.** If it's just a joke, then it's okay to make someone feel uncomfortable or cross their boundaries.

Worksheet 4.6.2

Directions: Because of our beliefs, we might sometimes feel like we have to say yes (or that we're supposed to say yes) in certain situations. When has saying no been hard for you? When have you felt like you have to say yes?

Read the following list of beliefs. Find three beliefs that have made it harder for you to say no. Share your experiences in the spaces provided.

- If I'm at someone's house, I believe (or sometimes believe) I can't say no to them.

- If someone's at my house, I believe (or sometimes believe) I can't say no to them.

- If someone was kind to me, hosted me, or gave me a gift, I believe (or sometimes believe) I can't say no to them.

- If someone is sad, I believe (or sometimes believe) I can't say no to them.

- If I love someone, I believe (or sometimes believe) I can't say no to them.

- If I said yes to them last time, I believe (or sometimes believe) I can't say no to them this time.

- If I might want to do the activity another time, even though I don't want to do it this time, I believe (or sometimes believe) I can't say no to them this time.

- If they are an authority figure like a teacher, religious leader, or babysitter, I believe (or sometimes believe) I can't say no to them.

- If we made plans ahead of time, I believe (or sometimes believe) I can't change my mind.

- If it was originally my idea, I believe (or sometimes believe) I can't change my mind.

1. **The belief:**

   When has this belief made it hard to say no in your life? Share your experience.

2. **The belief:**

   When has this belief made it hard to say no in your life? Share your experience.

3. **The belief:**

   When has this belief made it hard to say no in your life? Share your experience.

Because of My Position, Saying No Is Hard

Learning Objectives:

By the end of this lesson, students will be able to:

1. Define *position* (in terms of social position).

2. Describe how a person's position changes across circumstances.

3. Demonstrate an awareness of how position impacts a person's comfort in saying no and ignoring a no.

4. Identify ways they can use their position to help others feel valued and heard.

Time: 55 minutes

Materials:

- The flip chart you created in lesson 4.5
- Worksheet 4.7.1
- Worksheet 4.7.2
- Worksheet 4.7.3
- Whiteboard
- Whiteboard markers

Before You Start:

- Read through the lesson plan.
- Print worksheet 4.7.1 (one per student).
- Print worksheet 4.7.2 (one per student).
- Print worksheet 4.7.3 (one per student).

Note: While this lesson addresses social positioning and touches on concepts like identity and power, there is much more learning to be done that doesn't fall within the scope of this curriculum but impacts how students will understand and practice consent. The appendix has recommendations for classroom resources.

Step 1   Introduce the Topic

Hang the flip chart your class created during lesson 4.5 at the front of the classroom.

Guide the class in taking two deep breaths.

"In the last two sessions, we've spoken about how our beliefs can make saying no hard and how other people's words and actions can make saying no hard. Today, we're going to explore how a person's position can make saying no hard."

Ask the class if they know what the word *position* means.

"*Position* can describe a person's job on a team. In baseball, you might ask a person what position they play. *Position* can also refer to how something is arranged. You might tell the person in charge of building your house that you want the front door to be in a position where it's easy to get to from the kitchen.

"We're going to use the word *position* to talk about how *people* are positioned. Specifically, how people can be positioned as more important or less important, as mattering more or mattering less. In this lesson, we're going to explore how the way people *see us* and how we *see ourselves* can impact our consent practices."

Step 2   Discussion

Write the following on the board:

> My consent practice will be influenced by how I'm positioned in this situation. → My consent practice will be influenced by how I'm seen by others, and how I see myself, in this situation.

Then read the following to story to illustrate this concept:

"Ms. Sandra is a sixth grade teacher. Her students admire her. They're often impressed by her knowledge and experience. But, if we're being honest, they're also a little intimidated by her. They know that she's the person who writes their report cards, has a role in deciding what they learn, and is generally just 'in charge' of the class.

"Last week, Ms. Sandra was having a hard day. When her student, Asaf, asked her if he was allowed to doodle after he finished his worksheet, Ms. Sandra said no. When Asaf asked why, Ms. Sandra remarked, 'Because I'm the teacher and I said so.' Asaf didn't respond. He just sulked as he walked back to his seat.

"That evening, Ms. Sandra went to her parents' house. Her family was having dinner together in celebration of her dad's birthday. Ms. Sandra has two parents and four older brothers, making her the youngest in the family. Even though they're all adults, Ms. Sandra's brothers and parents still see her as the baby of the family.

"After the family sang 'Happy Birthday,' Ms. Sandra's dad asked Brian, the oldest child, to cut the cake. When Ms. Sandra asked Brian to cut her a piece with a frosting flower on it, Brian ignored her. He handed her a flowerless slice and scoffed, 'You get what you get.' Ms. Sandra rolled her eyes and quietly ate her cake.

"It was on Ms. Sandra's drive home, thinking about the incident with her brother, that she recognized her mistake earlier that day. Ms. Sandra started to see how she's positioned in her classroom versus how she's positioned at home and how this difference impacted her choices.

"In her family home, Ms. Sandra is just Sandra. Her family doesn't view her as especially admirable, knowledgeable, or in charge. Because of how her family sees her and because of how her brothers sometimes treat her, it's easy for Ms. Sandra to question whether her voice, her desires, and her boundaries matter.

"In Ms. Sandra's classroom, it's a different story. The people around her see her as knowledgeable and admirable, and as the most important person in the room. This makes it easier for Ms. Sandra to see herself that way. It gives her that feeling that her voice, her desires, and her boundaries matter.

"Brian treated Ms. Sandra like her perspective didn't matter in a similar way to how she treated her student Asaf. And just like Ms. Sandra had a hard time advocating for, or speaking up for, her perspective at home, Asaf had a hard time advocating for his perspective in the classroom."

DISCUSSION QUESTIONS:

- Why is Ms. Sandra more confident in the classroom than with her family?

    - *Talking points:* In the classroom, she's viewed by others and views herself as important and as someone whose perspective matters. It's easier to feel like you matter when other people act like you matter. At home, she's seen as the baby of the family whose perspective doesn't matter. It's hard to feel confident when the people around you treat you like you're less-than.

- In general, do you think it's easier for a person to say no to their younger sibling or to their teacher? Why?

    - *Talking points:* It is often harder to say no to people who are positioned as more important (as smarter, as more popular, as more trustworthy, or as mattering more for some other reason). This can be driven by a fear of consequences, a desire for approval, or a feeling of mattering less.

- What's the difference between being positioned as being more important and actually being more important?

  ○ *Talking points:* No one is a more important human than anyone else. We all matter. We all have value. We don't get to rank who is "worth" more as a person. All of our perspectives matter. Sometimes a person is *positioned* as more important because they have more knowledge, expertise, leadership skills, or experience in a certain area, and turning to that person for decision-making can help the whole group succeed. Sometimes, however, a person is positioned as more important because of how wealthy they are, how they look, how old they are, or how popular they are. Whether a person is seen as more important because of reasons like knowledge and expertise or reasons like appearance and age, that person needs to recognize how they are seen so that they can make sure not to take advantage of the situation, or of anyone in the situation.

- In our world, who is typically considered more important or seen as mattering more? (You can start students off with some suggestions if they're struggling to answer).

  ○ *Talking points:* Students might say: adults, tall people, boys, White people, people without disabilities, people with money, people with fancy jobs, and so on. Focus on what students bring up and what is relevant to them. If they only name people in authority positions, you might decide to mention how appearance, gender, class, ethnicity, and other factors play a role, or you might not. Either way, the goal isn't to dive deeply into any one of these identities and the way it impacts social perception and power. Rather, the goal is to give credence to the reality that, in our world, certain people are treated as more important than others. The aim here is to validate students who feel certain power dynamics in their everyday lives.

  ○ If you have already covered lessons on power and identity, you can refer back to these lessons.

  ○ If you've had training in talking about identity and power, and you have the time, you can use some of that knowledge here and dive deeper into how students' individual experiences have been shaped by social perception and power.

  ○ If this is a topic you don't feel prepared to dive into, that's totally okay! I still encourage you to ask this question and see what comes up without needing to go deep. If a student says that boys/men are treated as more important, you can validate that by pointing out the wage gap. Then move onto the next. If a student says that people with light skin are treated as mattering more, you can validate that by pointing to the makeup industry or Band-Aids and the options for lighter-skinned people compared to darker-skinned people. Then move on to the next. For lessons specifically about identity and power, see the recommendations in the appendix.

Step 3   Activity

Introduce worksheet 4.7.1 to the class and review the instructions. Remind students that these worksheets are for their eyes only. Give students about three minutes to complete the worksheet. Once students have completed it, ask the following questions.

DISCUSSION QUESTIONS:

- What are the biggest reasons why it's challenging for you to say no to someone who's positioned as more important?

  - *Talking points:* Take note of which items from worksheet 4.7.1 stand out.

- Why might it be easier to ignore someone's no when you hold a higher position or are seen as more important in some way?

  - *Talking points:* The reasons why it's hard to say no when you're positioned one way are also the reasons why it can become easy to ignore a no when you're positioned the other way. When you're seen as more important, you don't have to worry as much about not fitting in or making someone else feel upset. The world tells you that in this situation, you matter more. Think back to Ms. Sandra. She was quick to overlook her student's perspective at school, and he was pretty quick to accept her response. Meanwhile, at her family home, Ms. Sandra's brother was quick to overlook her perspective.

- Is it possible for you to be seen by others as more important, or in a high position, without realizing that people see you this way?

  - *Talking points:* Definitely. But it's much easier to recognize this when your perspective *isn't* seen as important. That's why Ms. Sandra only realized how she treated her student once she was treated in a similar way. This is why we need to pay attention to how we're seen. We need to pay attention to how we are positioned in certain situations and how that position can influence our consent practices and others' consent practices.

"Let's explore how a person can make caring and respectful decisions based on their position."

Introduce worksheet 4.7.2 to the class and review the instructions. You can also complete the worksheet together as a class. Give students about three minutes to complete the worksheet. Once students have completed it, review the answers together. Then ask the following questions.

DISCUSSION QUESTIONS:

- What stands out to you about the possible actions we can take?

  - *Talking points:* Take note of what students observe.

- Is it bad to be in a position where people see you as more important or mattering more?

  - *Talking points:* No. You don't really get to choose how people see you. However, you do get to choose what you do with this. As we see from these examples, you can use your position to focus only on your boundaries, desires, and goals—or you can use your position to make sure everyone is heard and that decisions are made collaboratively. It's not bad that Ms. Sandra is seen as important in her classroom; it helps keep the classroom running smoothly and helps the learning get done! Her students don't have to worry about that because she takes on that responsibility. However, she also needs to make sure that she's hearing her students' perspectives when making decisions because their boundaries, desires, and goals matter too. It's not a bad thing to be positioned, or seen, as more popular or more knowledgeable about a certain topic. What matters is how you treat people when you are in that position. Remember, being positioned or seen a certain way doesn't mean that you are a certain way.

Introduce worksheet 4.7.3 to the class. Review the instructions. Give students about five minutes to complete the worksheet. Once students have completed it, invite them to share what they noticed (without naming names).

DISCUSSION QUESTIONS:

- How did it feel to reflect on those situations? Was it easier to think of a time when it was hard for *you* to say no or a time when it was probably hard for *someone else* to say no to you? Why do you think that is?

  ○ *Talking points:* It's often easier to notice how you feel than how another person feels. That's why we each have to put effort into considering how someone might feel by paying attention to their body language and asking them questions. It's also hard for humans to think of themselves as being hard to say no to. But depending on our position, we can, without realizing it, be hard to say no to.

- When you are positioned in a way where it might be harder for someone to share their perspective with you, what can you do to make it easier for them to share their desires and boundaries?

  ○ *Talking points:* (Refer back to lesson 2.3.) Remind the other person that they can say no, remind them that you want to hear their real answers, check in with them during the interaction, ask them questions when coming up with a plan so they have space for their input, and so on.

"We will all make judgments about others based on who they are, what they look like, and what they appear to have. Just think about the assumptions we make about people we see on social media and how easy it is to think that they're cool or rich or have all the answers. Our judgments can influence how we feel about other people, about ourselves, and about who we should listen to. We need to actively notice these judgments, including how we see others, how we see the situation, and how others might see us. From there, we can do what we can to make sure that everyone feels valued and that everyone's perspective is heard. It's the job of the person who's positioned as more important to make it easier for others to share their perspective. That's the responsibility that comes with that position."

Conclude the lesson by explaining, "Even the best boundary-setters have a hard time saying no at times. If we have trouble saying no, it's not because we're weak or pushovers, but because saying no is hard and is something that takes practice."

Model It

- Recognize your position.

  - Position and social power exist, and that's not a bad thing. It's possible to abuse power, but it's also possible to use our power to empower—to use our authority, experience, and knowledge to lift others up and give them more power, choice, knowledge, and experience. The first step in empowering others is recognizing our ability to do so. For example, when you recognize that you have insight that a student doesn't have, rather than making a decision for them because you "know more," you can empower them by teaching them, coaching them, and supporting them in their decision-making. Once you reflect on your position and power, you can make choices that support empowerment.

- Consider what your actions communicate about positionality and power.

  - As teachers, we model for students what it means to have power or to be in a position where we are socially valued or seen as more important. When you say "Because I said so," students learn that the person with more power gets to make the rules for everyone. When you say "You're overreacting," students learn that it's okay for people in power to invalidate others' emotions. When you say "I'm sorry you're so sensitive," students learn that the person in power doesn't really need to be responsible for their words and actions. We want to show our young people that being positioned as important doesn't exempt someone from showing care and consideration. In fact, it's even more important that people in these positions do so. You have an opportunity to show your students how to be responsible with position and power.

Coach It

- Coach students to consider their position.

  - Because kids are so used to not having power and being a position with low authority and esteem, they can easily lose sight of how much power they do have in a situation. When conflict between students arises and students' positions seem to be playing a role, you can address it. It's best to (1) do this once you see a pattern and (2) describe the situation, behaviors, and feelings rather than the power dynamics or hierarchies at play.

1. Wait to see a pattern:

   – When you notice a student lacking awareness of their position
     or making use of it in a way that is inconsiderate to others,
     and if the stakes are relatively low, there are a couple of reasons
     you might decide to let the situation play out. First, it allows
     space for them to correct themselves. Second, it allows space
     for another student to call it out and try to navigate the conflict
     themselves. We don't want to take either of these opportunities
     away from students too quickly. Third, it might be a one-time
     thing. Perhaps that student had a hard day or is feeling hangry.
     This isn't an excuse for them to be inconsiderate. However,
     you want to make sure that you're having the appropriate
     conversation with them. You might still decide to speak
     with them about how they navigated the situation, but the
     conversation won't be driven by the impact of positionality as
     much as by curiosity about what specifically happened.

   – Letting the situation play out allows you to address the student
     when you have more time. Speaking with a student outside of
     a situation gives more room for back-and-forth. Imagine that a
     very popular student, Natalie, is unilaterally deciding the rules
     of a game. She might not realize how popular she is or the role
     that her position plays in other students' decision-making. If
     you speak with Natalie outside of the situation, there's time for
     a longer conversation, which means more space for Natalie to
     come to certain realizations on her own.

2. Describe the situation, behaviors, and feelings rather than the power
   dynamics or hierarchies at play.

   – Labeling isn't a great strategy for learning and growing. Describing
     behaviors and feelings is the way to go. Using the situation with
     Natalie as an example, you might ask Natalie to consider how
     many friends she has or whether she's ever nervous about not
     having someone to sit with during lunch or play with during
     recess. You can indirectly address how others might feel about
     her. You can point out that not all students have that experience,
     so they might look up to her. From there, the two of you can
     brainstorm how Natalie can use this gift to make future situations
     a fun experience for everyone.

- Empathize with students when they're having trouble saying no because of how they're positioned.

  ○ You can also use the reality of position and power to validate why a student is saying yes to things they don't want to do and no to things they do want to do. Use a personal anecdote to demonstrate that being in a certain position can make it harder for anyone to say no. From there, you can see if they're interested in practical advice.

Worksheet 4.7.1

When someone is positioned as *more important* than others in a situation, or seen as mattering more, it can become easier for them to focus on themselves and ignore *others'* desires and boundaries.

When someone is positioned as *less important* than others in a situation, or seen as mattering less, it can become easier for them to focus on others and ignore *their own* desires and boundaries.

Directions: Listed below are some reasons why it can be hard to say no or share your boundaries with people who are positioned as more important. Put a check mark next to any reasons that explain why it's hard to say no or share your boundaries with people who are positioned as more important. Share any additional reasons in the blank spaces.

Saying no can be hard for me because . . .

- ❏ I get nervous they won't like me.
- ❏ I get nervous about what they'll do if I say no.
- ❏ I don't want to make them mad.
- ❏ I don't want to make them sad.
- ❏ I want to fit in.
- ❏ I get scared they'll take it out on me later.
- ❏ I feel like my limits aren't important.
- ❏ I fear that other people will judge me for saying no to that person.
- ❏ I don't want to let them down.
- ❏ I'm just so used to saying yes to people in higher positions.
- ❏ I get nervous I'll be the only one speaking up and going against what everyone else wants.
- ❏ I depend on them for something (grades, friendship, support, food, or other things).
- ❏ I don't want to get into a conflict or fight with someone who's seen as mattering more.
- ❏ I feel like what I want (or don't want) doesn't matter as much.
- ❏ I'm worried they won't listen to me anyway, so why bother?
- ❏ I can't explain it. It's just hard.
- ❏ _____
- ❏ _____

Worksheet 4.7.2

When someone is positioned as mattering more or as more important, they can use their position to help others or to hurt others.

Directions: For each of the following scenarios, circle the action that would help others and cross out the action that would hurt others.

Situation	Action A	Action B
You are seen as bigger and stronger than them.	You offer your help when they might want it. You protect them when necessary.	You pick on them. You do what you want to them without their permission.
You are seen as more experienced or skilled.	You tease them for their mistakes. You publicly share their struggles. You gloat about your skills.	You support their learning journey with encouragement. You remind yourself, and them, that we can all learn from each other.
You are seen as more popular.	You make the decisions for the group because everyone will listen to you.	Because people listen to you, you use your voice to make sure everyone has a turn to speak and everyone's perspective is considered.
You are seen as more innocent.	You make sure that you take responsibility for your actions.	You let others take the blame for your mistakes because you know there's a good chance that you'll get away with your actions.

Worksheet 4.7.3

Directions: Take a moment to consider your position in different situations, including in our classroom, our school, your friend group, your sports team, your family, and your community.

1. Share a time when because of how you were positioned, it was harder for you to say no.

2. Share a time when because of how you were positioned, it was probably harder for someone to say no to you.

I Do My Part in Caring for the Both of Us

When They Mess Up

Time:
35 minutes

Learning Objectives:

By the end of this lesson, students will be able to:

1. Identify the reasons a person might not respect a no.

2. Demonstrate several strategies for responding to situations in which someone isn't respecting their boundaries.

3. Demonstrate compassion for themselves (and others) when they aren't fully upfront about their boundaries.

Materials:

*   Handout 5.1.1
*   Script 5.1.1
*   Script 5.1.2
*   Whiteboard
*   Whiteboard markers

Before You Start:

*   Read through the lesson plan.
*   Print handout 5.1.1 (one per student).
*   Print script 5.1.1. (two copies).
*   Print script 5.1.2. (two copies).

Step 1   Introduce the Topic

Guide the class in taking two deep breaths.

"It's impossible to never have your boundaries crossed and to never cross someone else's boundaries. Maybe you play music too loudly for someone's comfort, or maybe a friend pokes you in your side when you're not in the mood.

"Whether it was by accident or on purpose, when a friend crosses a boundary of yours or pressures you to say yes, you get to share your concerns, ask for an apology or accountability (we'll talk more about this later), and take space away from them if you need. This is what we're going to talk about today. We're going to explore what to do when someone messes up in their consent practice by pressuring you or by crossing a boundary."

Before moving on, review any past child sexual abuse prevention lessons or discussions you've had outside of this curriculum. Make it clear that this lesson refers to common mistakes and mess-ups in friendships, not to unsafe adult-child or child-child behavior.

Step 2 Discussion

"You might cross a friend's boundaries, or a friend might cross yours. Sometimes it will be by accident, and sometimes it will be on purpose."

Invite students to name reasons why a friend might ignore their no. Generate a list on the board.

Your list might look something like:

- They didn't hear you.

- They didn't want you to say no.

- They think they can get away with ignoring your no.

- They hope you'll give up on your boundaries once it's already happening.

- They don't care about your boundaries.

- They think you're being unfair.

DISCUSSION QUESTIONS:

- Is it okay to ignore someone's no for any of the reasons listed on the board?

    ○ *Talking points:* It's not okay, *and* it doesn't make the person a bad person. We are working under the assumptions that there are no bad people, just people who in a moment did something that wasn't okay. That person needs to work on how not to let that happen again and how to create repair now (something we'll talk about in the next lesson).

- How would you feel if you told a friend that you needed personal space and didn't want a hug, but your friend hugged you anyway? (You can also ask how they would feel if they told a sibling that the sibling couldn't borrow their sweatshirt but then the sibling borrowed it anyway.)

    ○ *Talking points:* Discuss the feelings of violation, betrayal, discomfort, distrust, and more that they might feel. Tie this back to the importance of recognizing what they have a right to and what they don't have a right to.

"When someone makes a mistake, they might quickly realize their mistake, they might keep trying to push your boundary, or they might just cross it, even though you've said no. We're going to review some things you can say when someone isn't respecting your no or keeps pushing you to do to what they want."

Tell your class that you will be doing a call-and-repeat. You will say a statement, and their job is to repeat it. First you will review statements for when someone is being pushy or pressuring you to do what they want (e.g., "Let me borrow your toy"). Then you'll review statements for when someone has crossed the boundary that's already been set (e.g., takes your toy without asking or ignores your no).

RESPONSES FOR WHEN SOMEONE IS BEING PUSHY AND PRESSURING:

- "You asked. I said no."

- "I already gave you my answer."

- "I said no, and my boundaries deserve respect."

- "If you do that, you will be crossing my boundary."

- "This is a decision I get to make, and I said no."

- "This is a decision I get to make. Please stop trying to change my mind."

RESPONSES FOR WHEN SOMEONE HAS ALREADY CROSSED A BOUNDARY:

- "Stop what you're doing. I said no."

- "You're crossing my boundary, and that's not okay."

- "I said no and you're doing it anyway. Please stop."

- "I'm not okay with what you're doing. Please stop, and ask me first next time."

Lead three call-and-repeats for each statement. For the first two, use bigger energy so that students really feel the power of owning their boundary. Before the third time, remind them how assertiveness is a way of sharing a boundary that is kind to both oneself and others. Take a deep breath. Prompt them to deliver the third response in a calm, strong, "indoor" voice.

To conclude the activity, hand each student a copy of handout 5.1.1 and discuss the following with the class:

- How did that feel?

- Which phrases can you see yourself using in real-life moments?

- Will it be as easy to say these phrases when you're actually being pressured? If not, what can you do to find the courage to respond?

  - *Talking points:* They can take a deep breath, practice self-affirmations, or find support in a teacher or trusted adult. Remind students that responding to pressure can be challenging, and it's okay if they struggle to say these phrases. The goal is to work toward getting more comfortable and more practiced at setting and maintaining boundaries. The goal isn't to stand up assertively every single time. No one can do that. Depending on the situation and how we are feeling, some days it will be easier and some days it will be harder.

- What will you do if you hear someone say one of these statements to you?

  - *Talking points:* Ideally, students will stop what they are doing, recognize their boundary violation, and try to repair the situation. We'll talk about this more deeply in lesson 5.3.

Step 4   Skits

"So far, we've reviewed how you can respond with words when someone is pressuring you or when they cross your boundary. But words aren't your only option. There are actions you can take in these moments too."

Invite students to help in performing two short skits. If no students are interested in volunteering, ask another teacher to perform with you.

SKIT #1:

Select two volunteer students. Hand each student a copy of script 5.1.1.

Set the scene: Two students are hanging out during recess. Call "Action!" to tell students to begin their performance.

When the scene is over, lead a round of applause. Then discuss the following, replacing *Student A* and *Student B* with the students' actual names:

- [Student A] was pressuring [Student B] to share their phone. [Student B] said no and then restated their answer. When [Student A] didn't respect their named limits, how did [Student B] take action to keep themselves and their stuff protected?

  ○ *Talking points:* Student B left the situation. They moved themselves to another location, away from the person who was pressuring them. This can be a powerful way to respond when someone is not practicing consent well.

- What else might you say to someone so that you can leave a conversation or situation where your boundaries aren't being respected?

  ○ *Talking points:* You can tell them you need to use the bathroom, get water, check on something, fulfill a prior commitment (do something you said you were going to do), or take time to yourself.

SKIT #2:

Select two volunteer students. Hand each student a copy of script 5.1.2.

Set the scene: Two students are hanging out during recess. Call "Action!" to tell students to begin their performance.

When the scene is over, lead a round of applause. Then discuss the following, replacing *Student A* and *Student B* with the students' actual names:

- [Student A] was pressuring [Student B] to share their phone. [Student B] said no and then restated their answer. When [Student A] didn't respect their named limits, how did [Student B] take action to keep themselves and their stuff protected?

  ○ *Talking points:* They called on a trusted person for support. In situations like this where no one is in immediate danger, you might want to call on a close friend for support (as they did in the skit). For situations that are more dangerous or when you don't feel comfortable asking a friend for support, you can also seek help from an adult. (This is also a time to refer back to your child sexual abuse prevention lessons and the importance of talking to safe adults.)

- If a friend or an adult isn't nearby, what are some ways you can leave the conversation to get to one?

  ○ *Talking points:* Use the same strategies talked about already (water, bathroom, and so on), and when you've stepped away, find the help you need.

Ask students to use a show of hands to share if they've ever said "Maybe later" when they really wanted to say no or when someone kept pressuring them after they'd said no.

"In general, we want to be honest about our boundaries. If you never want a hug from someone, it's generally not best to say, 'Not now, but maybe later.' However, when someone is pressuring you or you have real reason to believe they won't accept your no, it's okay to use this strategy or similar ones to keep yourself and your boundaries protected. If you realize they actually are a safe person to be honest with, you can always return to them to share that you weren't totally truthful and explain the reasons *why* you weren't totally truthful.

"Let's look at an example. Your friend invites you for a sleepover. Just thinking about a sleepover makes you nervous. You don't want to sleep away from home, but you don't want to share this information because you are nervous about how the friend will respond. When you decline the invitation, you tell your friend, 'Sorry, I'm busy that day.' Now, that's not really true, and we can understand why you might say that. Later, when you are feeling calmer, if you realize you *can* trust this friend, you can tell them the real reason you didn't say yes and explain to them how your fears and stress in the moment played a role."

DISCUSSION QUESTIONS:

- What are your thoughts on this situation?
    - *Talking points:* There's no right answer. It's okay for different students to have different reactions.

- Is it okay not to be honest about the reason you're saying no? When is it okay, and when is it not okay?
    - *Talking points:* The goal here is to help students understand that these situations are difficult to navigate. That means we do our best to be gentle with ourselves when trying to figure out what to say *and* to be gentle with others when we find out that a friend was afraid to share the whole story.

- Is it okay to be mad that someone didn't tell you the whole truth?
    - *Talking points:* Yes. It's okay to have feelings or anger or hurt. We also have to be responsible for our feelings and do our best not to let them lead us to yelling or calling a friend a mean name. We can both be hurt or mad *and* try to be compassionate. We'll talk more about how to work through a mess-up like this in a coming lesson.

Supporting This Lesson in Your Classroom's Culture

Model It

- Use these strategies yourself.

  ○ If a student requests to sit on your lap and you say no, but they keep pushing you, you can use some of the phrases shared in the lesson. You can say "I said no. Please respect my body boundaries" or "This a decision I'm not willing to collaborate on. The answer is no." Assertively sharing your boundaries models for your students how to do the same.

  ○ That being said, because the power dynamic between you and your students favors you, be mindful of how their boundary mistakes (e.g., pressuring you or not asking you) impact you versus how your boundary mistakes (e.g., pressuring them or not asking them) impact them. You, as the adult, have more power than them. As an educator, it's your job to empower, collaborate, and reinforce students' right to have a say in the decisions that impact them.

Coach It

- Support students in reaffirming their boundaries.

  ○ You can step in and say to the student being pressured (within earshot of the other student), "I heard you say no three times. Sounds like you're a no, yeah?" Feeding them some boundary phrases can be a real gift.

  ○ You can say to the other student, "I heard them say no. It sounds like you have your answer."

  ○ You can see if the students are willing to collaborate and help facilitate that skill.

  ○ You can also start with a curiosity about collaboration and flex into reinforcing the original no.

  ○ You also might let it play out a little longer to see if they can figure it out themselves.

  ○ How you respond will be context dependent. Who the students are, where they are in their learning journeys, what the conflict is about, and what the power dynamics between the two students are will all impact your choice. There are many possible right answers in these situations.

Handout 5.1.1

There are several things you can say when someone isn't respecting your no or keeps pushing you to do what they want.

Responses for when they are being pushy and pressuring:

- "You asked. I said no."
- "I already gave you my answer."
- "I said no, and my boundaries deserve respect."
- "If you do that, you will be crossing my boundary."
- "This is a decision I get to make, and I said no."
- "This is a decision I get to make. Please stop trying to change my mind."

Responses for when they have already crossed a boundary:

- "Stop what you're doing. I said no."
- "You're crossing my boundary, and that's not okay."
- "I said no and you're doing it anyway. Please stop."
- "I'm not okay with what you're doing. Please stop, and ask me first next time."

Script 5.1.1

STUDENT A: Hey, can I play with your phone?

STUDENT B: No, I don't let anyone borrow my phone.

STUDENT A: C'mon it's not a big deal.

STUDENT B: You asked. I said no.

STUDENT A: But I'll be so careful.

STUDENT B: Maybe another time. I'm gonna go see what Mickey and Shira are up to.

Student B walks away

Script 5.1.2

STUDENT A: Hey, can I play with your phone?

STUDENT B: No, I don't let anyone borrow my phone.

STUDENT A: C'mon it's not a big deal.

STUDENT B: I already gave you my answer.

STUDENT A: But I'll be so careful. Just let me do one thing.
It'll be so quick.

Student B turns to imaginary person

STUDENT B: Hey, Mickey, can you help me remind [student A's name] that no means no?

Is It Clarification, Encouragement, or Pressure?

Time:
35 minutes

Learning Objectives:

By the end of this lesson, students will be able to:

1. Describe the differences between clarifying information, encouraging someone, and pressuring someone.

2. Identify when to use (and not use) these behaviors.

3. Demonstrate how to recognize these behaviors in action.

Materials:

- Worksheet 5.2.1

- Whiteboard

- Whiteboard markers

Before You Start:

- Read through the lesson plan.

- Decide which option in step 3 best suits your class. If students will complete the worksheet on their own, print worksheet 5.2.1 (one per student).

Step 1   Introduce the Topic

Guide the class in taking two deep breaths.

"By now, we have a strong understanding of why it's important to respect a no and why pressuring someone into changing their decision isn't okay. Today, we're going to talk about the difference between pressuring, encouraging, and clarifying information."

Write the words *encouraging*, *pressuring*, and *clarifying information* on the board.

"Let's examine a story with three different endings." Read the following story and each of the three endings.

Story: "Rebecca is on a trip with her family. The day's activity is ziplining. They're going to hike up a mountain. Then, one by one, after being securely attached to a cable, they'll slide along the cable and over trees. They'll eventually touch down safely on a landing across the way."

Ending 1: "Rebecca gets to the top of the mountain and starts shaking. 'I'm so nervous,' she says. 'This looks so scary.' Rebecca's dad tries to reassure her. 'C'mon, sweetie,' he says, 'it'll be fun.' But it doesn't look fun to Rebecca. She exclaims, 'No, there is no way I'm doing this!' Rebecca's dad lets out a big sigh. 'Rebecca, we climbed all the way up here. Don't chicken out now. You're going ruin it for your siblings.'"

Ask students how they would describe the dad's response and how it might make Rebecca feel. Then read on.

Ending 2: "Rebecca gets to the top of the mountain and starts shaking. 'I'm so nervous,' she says. 'This looks so scary.' Rebecca's dad tries to reassure her. 'It is quite high up; I see why you're feeling nervous.' Rebecca responds, 'I want to swing down, but it looks so intense!' Rebecca's dad agrees, 'It does look intense. I believe in you, though. If you want to do it, I know you can do it!' Rebecca takes some deep breaths. Rebecca's dad rubs her back and replies, 'It's okay to be scared. I think it looks fun and scary too. You don't have to get over your fears to do it. If you want to, you *can* do it scared. You climbed all the way up. I think you can do it.'"

Ask students how they would describe the dad's response and how it might make Rebecca feel. Then read on.

Ending 3: "Rebecca gets to the top of the mountain and starts shaking. 'I'm so nervous,' she says. 'This looks so scary.' Rebecca's dad nods his head and says, 'It is pretty high up.' Rebecca agrees, 'It seriously is. I don't want to go. When I get scared my palms sweat. What if I accidentally let go of the line?' Rebecca's dad smiles. 'That's what the harness is for,' he says. Rebecca looks at her dad with confusion. Her dad continues, 'You'll be securely strapped into a harness, so even if you let go, there's no way you can fall. If you could, that would be much too dangerous.'" Rebecca lets out an *ohhh* followed by 'Then what are we waiting for? Let's do it!'"

Ask students how they would describe the dad's response and how it might make Rebecca feel.

Summarize their answers, naming each of the dad's approaches in responding to Rebecca: in the first story, Dad was pressuring her, in the second he was encouraging her, and in the third he was clarifying information for her.

Discuss the differences between the three:

- "When someone shows disinterest in an activity and you try to get them to say yes anyway, you are probably *pressuring* them."

- "When someone shows interest in an activity and you try to help them feel comfortable in their yes, you are probably *encouraging* them."

- "When someone makes a decision without having all of the facts and you try to share more information with them so that they can make a decision with the information they need, you are probably *clarifying information*."

DISCUSSION QUESTIONS:

- If someone says no to you, might it be okay to pressure them, encourage them, or clarify information for them?

  - *Talking points:* It can be okay to encourage and to clarify information. It isn't okay to pressure them.

- Why isn't it okay to pressure someone?

  - *Talking points:* Refer to all the information and conversations from lesson 4.5. "When you pressure someone, you are telling them, 'What I want is more important than what you want.' And while it might feel like that's true, we know it's not."

- Why is it okay to encourage someone? Can it ever not be okay to encourage? How can you know if someone wants encouragement?

  - *Talking points:* When we are encouraging, we are letting the other person lead. We are following their interests, not trying to make them agree to our interests. That being said, sometimes a person might not want encouragement. The best way to know if someone wants encouragement from you is to ask them.

- Why is it okay to clarify information? Is it possible to do too much clarification? If yes, what would too much clarification look like?

  - *Talking points:* Clarifying information isn't about pushing a person to do what you want or what you think is best for them. When you clarify information, you are supporting a person in making a decision for themselves with the information they might need. Too much information can overwhelm a person or make them feel like you're trying to convince them. I use this rule of thumb when it comes to clarifying: no more than two pieces of information without them prompting me or asking me for that information. This helps keep me from accidentally falling into pressuring territory. I can always ask, "Do you have any questions?" or "Can I can clarify anything for you?" so that I can feel more confident that I'm not overstepping.

Step 3 Activity + Discussion

Introduce worksheet 5.2.1 to the class and review the instructions. (You can also complete this activity together as a class.) Give students about four minutes to complete the worksheet. Once students have completed it, review their responses. It's okay if there's disagreement. People have different interpretations in real life too!

DISCUSSION QUESTIONS:

- Was it challenging to categorize the statements? What stood out?

  - *Talking points:* There's no right answer. Some students will find this easier, and some will find this harder. If there is disagreement when reviewing the answers, it's because understanding the line between clarifying information, pressuring, and encouraging can be challenging.

- When you tell someone that now is their only chance, is that clarifying information or pressuring them to do it now?

  - *Talking points:* It could be either. It depends on if it's true, how it's said, and what the motive or goal is. Today might be the last day of my visit, so saying "It's gotta be today or it can't happen" might be clarifying information. Saying that same statement just to get my way, though, would be a form of pressuring.

- Is it always easy to tell the difference between pressuring, encouraging, and clarifying? If no, how can you make it easier for someone to see what your intentions are?

  - *Talking points:* It's not always easy to tell the difference. You can be clear about what you're trying to do by saying it out loud. You might say, "It sounds like you want to do this, so I want to encourage you. Do you want some encouragement right now?" or "I think you might not have the whole story. I'd like to share some details with you." You can also ask a person what their intentions are. You might say, "I think you're trying to encourage me, but it feels like pressure" or ask, "Are you trying to give me information right now or convince me to do it?" Communication is so valuable.

Supporting This Lesson in Your Classroom's Culture

Model It

- Recognize what your goals are and what their goals are.

  ○ Differentiating between your goals and a student's goals can help you recognize where your words of encouragement are actual encouragement and when you're actually in pressuring territory. When I was in high school, my physics teacher encouraged me to take the Advanced Placement (AP) B/C Physics course in my senior year. While I did well in his non-AP physics class, math wasn't my top subject and I wanted to have a more relaxed senior year. I knew that I would have to work really hard to succeed in the advanced class. I told him this, and he agreed that I would have to work hard but added that I was a great student and I could do it. While I was flattered that he believed in me, I really didn't want to take the class. I had other goals for my last year of high school. He was encouraging me, but it was based on his goals, not on mine.

  ○ Elementary school students don't usually get to pick what classes they take. When it comes to getting students to do schoolwork, sometimes your goal for a student won't be the same as their goal, and yet, the learning still has to happen. In these moments, don't resort to pressure. Instead, you can help students name their own goals and then encourage them in accomplishing those goals. Using their language instead of your language can help a student go from feeling pressured to feeling encouraged. You can also utilize the language of "willing" and "wanting" from lesson 3.2. See what they are willing to do. In these moments, it's not about encouraging them, pressuring them, or clarifying information for them. It's about you making a request and them being willing to fulfill it.

  ○ Ultimately, your goal here is to model for students that they get choice in decisions that impact them. The person in power doesn't get to make all decisions. By modeling that it's not okay for teachers to pressure or to give encouragement when encouragement isn't wanted, we show students that the role of the person in power is to empower others and help them choose what works for them.

Coach It

- Find out what they would choose.

  - If a child is scared to go down a slide, sign up for a difficult class, take on a big project, or try out for the basketball team, we do best by our students if we slow down and take the time to learn what choice they want to make and be supportive in helping them make it. If they don't want to try out for the team and need reassurance that it's okay to do that, we can give them that. If they want to try out for the team but are nervous and need reassurance that it's okay to do something while scared and they'll be okay, we can give them that too. They get to choose, and choice can be complicated and take time.

  - Similarly, when you notice that a student might be pressuring their peer, intervene with this in mind. Check to see if the student is clarifying information, encouraging their peer, or pressuring their peer. If they're encouraging their peer, support them in uncovering whether their friend is interested in being encouraged.

Worksheet 5.2.1

Directions: Consider whether each of these statements describes pressuring, encouraging, or clarifying information.

Remember:

- **Pressuring** describes when someone has shown disinterest in an activity and someone else tries to get them to say yes anyway.

- **Encouraging** describes when someone has shown interest in an activity and someone else tries to help them feel comfortable in their yes.

- **Clarifying information** describes when someone is making decision and someone else shares missing information with them so that they can make a more informed choice.

1. "All the people there will be people you know."   *Pressuring   Encouraging   Clarifying*

2. "I'm here to support you, if you want."   *Pressuring   Encouraging   Clarifying*

3. "Do you want a push?"   *Pressuring   Encouraging   Clarifying*

4. "It's not on Thursday, it's on Sunday."   *Pressuring   Encouraging   Clarifying*

5. "But you have to."   *Pressuring   Encouraging   Clarifying*

6. "I believe in you, and it's your choice!"   *Pressuring   Encouraging   Clarifying*

7. "Just so you know, the pool closes in five minutes."   *Pressuring   Encouraging   Clarifying*

8. "Everyone will be annoyed if you say no."   *Pressuring   Encouraging   Clarifying*

9. "Would you like me to persuade you?"   *Pressuring   Encouraging   Clarifying*

10. "The carnival is only in town until tomorrow."   *Pressuring   Encouraging   Clarifying*

11. "Ugh, c'mon, I'm probably gonna be busy later."   *Pressuring   Encouraging   Clarifying*

When I Mess Up

Time:
25 minutes

Learning Objectives:

By the end of this lesson, students will be able to:

1. Demonstrate compassion for themselves when they make mistakes in their consent practice.

2. Identify areas of their consent practice that they can work on.

3. Name ways to improve on common consent practice mistakes.

Materials:

- Worksheet 5.3.1

Before You Start:

- Read through the lesson plan.

- Print worksheet 5.3.1 (one per student).

Step 1   Introduce the Topic

Guide the class in taking two deep breaths.

"We've talked about what to do if someone isn't respecting your boundaries. Now we're going to talk about what to do if you realize that you're not respecting someone else's boundaries."

Remind students of the list they created in lesson 5.1 of reasons why someone might not respect a no. Review some of those reasons.

"Just like others might not respect a no, each of us is capable of getting caught up in not respecting a no for these reasons too. Today, we're going to talk about ways each of us might mess up in our consent practice, and next time we're going to talk about what we can do when that happens."

Ask students, "Aside from messing up by not respecting a no, how else might a person stumble in their consent practice? How might a person fall off course in their effort to navigate both their own desires and boundaries and another person's desires and boundaries?"

(You can give students a hint by suggesting they think about all of the skills you've discussed in the curriculum so far.)

Answers might include not asking first, not paying attention to the other person's body language, not checking in, and not handling a no well. These are all *interpersonal* mess-ups.

Answers might also include failing to pay attention to what your own body is saying, not sharing your desires, saying yes when you really want to say no, and not speaking up when you noticed you've had a change of heart. These are all *intrapersonal* mess-ups.

Because practicing consent involves guarding both people's desires and boundaries, it's important to recognize both categories of mess-ups and to improve in both categories. That being said, in this lesson, we will put more emphasis on interpersonal mistakes (the things we do that impact others).

Ask students whether it's okay to make these mistakes when practicing consent (or to veer off course in these ways). Then explain, "Consent is a practice, which means we're going to make mistakes. You're not a bad person for making mistakes—that's how you learn. It's an important part of the learning process."

Reinforce that while mistakes are common on both sides, we want to do our best to minimize them. If our consent mistakes are getting smaller and less frequent—if we're not repeating the same mistakes and we are working to recognize and change our mistakes more quickly—it means we're learning and growing, and that's a big win.

Introduce worksheet 5.3.1 to the class and review the instructions. Give students about four minutes to complete the worksheet. Let students know that this worksheet is for their eyes only so that they are free to be as honest as possible.

DISCUSSION QUESTIONS:

- How did it feel to think about your consent practice in this way?

  ◦ *Talking points:* There's no right answer. Listen to how students felt and what came up for them.

- Is it reasonable for anyone to mark themselves as "never" on every statement? Why not?

  ◦ *Talking points:* No, because we all make mistakes.

- If you marked "often" or "always" for any items, does that mean you're a bad person? Why not?

  ◦ *Talking points:* No, it means you have places where you can improve.

- What can you do with this information you now have about yourself?

  ◦ *Talking points:* Pay attention to these moments more, come up with a plan for doing better in these areas, try to do better in these areas, and ask for help in these skills.

Choose a few items from the worksheet to review. For each one, ask, "Why do you think a person might do this?" Encourage students to name both intentional and accidental reasons for these actions. Discuss their responses.

Then ask, "What are some things you can try to do in the future to learn and grow in this part of your consent practice?" Discuss their responses.

Supporting This Lesson in Your Classroom's Culture

Model It

- Label your own missteps.

  ○ One of the most powerful ways to help your students feel like they are in a safe learning environment is to acknowledge that you are still learning too. This means apologizing when you don't ask first, when you pressure, and when you reinforce myths like "Saying no is rude" or "You can't change your mind."

Coach It

- Reinforce that it's okay to mess up.

  ○ Keep in mind that without the space to get it wrong, we will never be able to get it right. One element missing from mainstream consent education is the lack of discussion and information on what to do when you mess up. As of this writing, I have yet to see a consent curriculum or talk to a school that touches on this element of practicing consent.

  ○ As teachers, we know that proficiency requires practice. Yet, so often, high school or college students are introduced to consent once or twice and then expected to get it right every time. If we actually want students to be proficient in navigating desire, agreement, touch, collaboration, and willingness, then we need them to practice now—before they're in high school and college—and we need to create a space where it's safe for them to mess up. We have so much power to help with that.

  ○ When a student messes up, emphasize that messing up is part of learning. Instead of punishing mistakes, support the opportunity for learning and accountability. We'll talk more about this in the next lesson.

Worksheet 5.3.1

Directions: Time to reflect on your consent practice. Take a moment to consider your past interactions. Then circle the option that best describes what you do most of the time.

1. I forget to pay attention to a friend or sibling's body language.

   Never   *Rarely*   *Sometimes*   *Often*   *Always*

2. I tell a friend or sibling that they're not allowed to change their mind.

   Never   *Rarely*   *Sometimes*   *Often*   *Always*

3. I make it hard for a friend or sibling to say no to me.

   Never   *Rarely*   *Sometimes*   *Often*   *Always*

4. I refuse to collaborate. I push to get my way.

   Never   *Rarely*   *Sometimes*   *Often*   *Always*

5. I make assumptions about someone's response instead of asking a clarifying question.

   Never   *Rarely*   *Sometimes*   *Often*   *Always*

6. I tell people what they have to do instead of asking them what they want to do.

   Never   *Rarely*   *Sometimes*   *Often*   *Always*

7. I push friends or siblings after they've said no.

   Never   *Rarely*   *Sometimes*   *Often*   *Always*

8. I insist that I'm okay with something even when I'm not.

   Never   *Rarely*   *Sometimes*   *Often*   *Always*

9. I notice the other person isn't having fun, but I don't check in on if they want to continue.

   Never   *Rarely*   *Sometimes*   *Often*   *Always*

10. I tell friends that it's rude to say no.

    Never   *Rarely*   *Sometimes*   *Often*   *Always*

11. I touch others or take their stuff without pausing to consider or ask how they may feel.

    Never   *Rarely*   *Sometimes*   *Often*   *Always*

12. I try to make friends, siblings, parents, or teachers feel bad about saying no.

    Never   *Rarely*   *Sometimes*   *Often*   *Always*

Responsibility and Accountability

Time: 60 minutes

Learning Objectives:

By the end of this lesson, students will be able to:

1. Describe the parts of accountability.

2. Identify behaviors that support accountability and behaviors that don't.

3. Recognize why it's possible for two people to be accountable.

4. Describe how blame and shame can get in the way of being responsible for one's actions.

5. Demonstrate how to apologize for their actions.

Materials:

- Worksheet 5.4.1
- Bell (optional)
- Whiteboard
- Whiteboard markers

Before You Start:

- Read through the lesson plan.
- Print worksheet 5.4.1 (one per student).
- Create three signs: one that reads "Blaming Others (not enough responsibility)"; one that reads "Shaming Self (too much responsibility)"; and one that reads "True Responsibility."

Step 1   Introduce the Topic

Guide the class in taking two deep breaths.

"In our last lesson, we spent time reflecting on how we can improve in our individual consent practices. Today, we're going to dive deeper into what we can do when we mess up in consent."

"Imagine you're in your kitchen, getting a snack from the cupboard. As you reach up, you knock over a cup of water that was sitting on the counter. Water spills everywhere. What might you do next?"

As you gather responses from the class, describe the many possible decisions a person in that situation can make. They can ignore it, clean it up, ask for help, demand help, try to find the person who left the cup there, or get stuck on how clumsy they must be.

Then say, "In a situation like this, you have many options. We're going to focus on the options that support something called accountability. Who knows what is means to be accountable?"

After students share their responses, say, "Being accountable means taking responsibility for your actions and doing what you can to repair the situation, show care in the relationship, and consider what you can do to lessen the chances that the same mistake happens again. We can think about accountability as having four parts."

Write the four parts of accountability on the board (Mingus, 2019):

1. Self-reflection

2. Apologizing

3. Repair (the relationship)

4. Behavior change

Review the meaning of each of these parts:

1. "The first part of accountability is self-reflection. This means asking yourself, 'What harm did my actions cause? How can I do better next time?'"

2. "The second part of accountability is apologizing. This means saying sorry and acknowledging the role you played in someone else's hurt."

3. "The third part is repair, or rebuilding trust. Depending on your relationship, repair might take more time and effort or less time and effort."

4. "The last part of accountability is behavior change. This means you continue to reflect on what got in the way and you make a commitment to not repeat the same behavior. You may even put some systems in place so the same thing is less likely to happen again."

"It's important to be accountable for big mistakes and small ones. In fact, being accountable for small mistakes is exactly what prepares us to be accountable for big ones. In this spilled-water scenario, even though the impact is relatively small, you still have an opportunity to be accountable."

You can either ask students to name how each part of accountability might look in the spilled-water scenario or sketch it out yourself with the following breakdown:

1. "Self-reflection might look like recognizing your role in spilling the water and how it might feel to have your drink spilled."

2. "You can apologize to the person whose cup it was and see how they are feeling."

3. "In this situation, the relationship may not need repair, but you can repair the situation by cleaning up the mess and refilling the cup. If the relationship does need repair (maybe because this is an ongoing problem and the other person is starting to feel like you don't care about their stuff), then you can work on rebuilding trust by tending to their needs and giving them space or closeness, depending on what would feel good to them."

4. "Last, you can put that refilled cup further from the edge of the counter and try to pay more attention to your surroundings the next time you're reaching for a snack."

If students push back and say that they shouldn't apologize because it was the fault of the person who left the water by the counter's edge, let them know you'll get back to this later on in the lesson.

"Just like in this example of spilling water, after you make a mistake or misstep in consent, you can be (and it's important to be) accountable too."

Step 3   Activity + Discussion

Introduce worksheet 5.4.1 to the class and review the instructions. Give students about four minutes to complete the worksheet. Once students have completed it, review their responses.

DISCUSSION QUESTIONS:

- What elements of accountability mean the most to you as someone who's been hurt?

    ○ *Talking points:* There's no right answer. For some people, hearing an apology might mean the most, while for others, hearing a commitment to do better in the future might mean the most.

- What parts of being accountable are harder for you? What makes accountability easier or harder for you?

  - *Talking points:* There are several factors that can play a role, including who it is, how you're feeling, and what the situation was.

- Does accountability always look the same? Does the process always take the same amount of time, energy, and effort? Why or why not?

  - *Talking points:* No, it doesn't always look the same. If a friend accidentally steps on your foot during tag and you're okay, a quick sorry might be enough. But if you knock them over and they hit the ground hard, a sorry might not be enough. If you accidentally step on friends' feet during tag on a regular basis, it might not be enough too. Different situations and different people call for different responses. If you're not sure what a situation requires, you can ask the person what would feel helpful to them, or you can talk to a teacher for guidance.

- Do you only need to apologize if you caused hurt or harm on purpose?

  - *Talking points:* No. In the scenario where you accidentally spill water that's close to the edge, a person absolutely can and should still apologize for knocking it over.

- Is it possible that two people would need to be accountable or apologize in a single situation? Why or why not?

  - *Talking points:* Definitely! In the scenario where you accidentally spill water that's close to the edge, you can apologize for knocking it over, and the other person can apologize for keeping their water close to the edge of the counter. You can share that you cleaned it up. They can thank you for doing so and commit to being more careful about where they put their stuff.

It's easy to believe that if you're right, I'm wrong, and if I'm right, you're wrong, but it's possible to recognize where you messed up *and* ask others to recognize where they messed up. We are all responsible for our own actions.

Draw the responsibility spectrum on the board:

Responsibility Spectrum

Blame	Accountability	Shame
Not enough	Just right	Too much

Read the following story and accompanying story endings:

Story: "Max and Colline are building a fort out of pillows and blankets when, all of a sudden, Max grabs a pillow and uses it to whack Colline in the back while yelling, 'Pillow fight!' Colline falls down, ruining the section of the fort she was just working on. She's frustrated, to say the least. She turns to Max, rhetorically asking, 'What was that for?'"

Ending 1: "In one story, Max responds, 'What's the big deal? You can't expect to build a fort and not be prepared for a pillow fight.'"

Ending 2: "In another story, Max responds, 'Oh my gosh, I'm so sorry. I'm the worst. I wasn't thinking. You probably never want to hang out with me again. I'm such a bad friend.'"

Ask students, "Do you think either of Max's responses shows good accountability or ownership of his actions? Why or why not?"

Gather students' responses and explain, "Part of accountability is taking responsibility for your actions. Max could use some improvement in both responses.

"In the first scenario, Max didn't take enough responsibility. He blamed Colline for not anticipating (or guessing) that he would hit her with a pillow. Instead of apologizing and recognizing it would have been better to ask first if she wanted a pillow fight, he responded by defending his actions and blaming the situation for his actions.

"In the second scenario, Max took on too much responsibility. He shamed his character and his inability to be a good friend. Rather than recognizing and apologizing for his actions, he made it all about how unfortunate the situation was for him, and he did not tend to Colline's feelings and the situation she was now in."

Tell students you'll talk more about this scenario in a moment. Then introduce them to the following short activity.

In this activity, you'll use some of the actions listed on worksheet 5.4.1 (and some new ones) to help students better understand the difference between too much responsibility and too little responsibility.

Instruct students to make their way to an open area of the classroom. Hang up signs in three different areas of the room labeled:

- Blaming Others (not enough responsibility)

- Shaming Self (too much responsibility)

- True Responsibility

After you read each action from the following list aloud, have students move to the area of the room that best describes the action. If there's disagreement among students, talk it out with them:

- I say, "I'm sorry."

- I say, "What I did isn't a big deal."

- I insist that I deserve to be punished for my actions because I'm not a good friend.

- I insist that you're overreacting.

- I blame myself and label myself a "horrible person."

- I remind myself that consent is a practice and I'm working on it.

- I ask you if you need space.

- I pretend nothing happened.

- I tell you I'll do anything to make it up to you, no limits.

- I tell you it's not my fault.

- I let you know I'm going to try harder to use my skills next time.

Students will be moving around in the next activity, so they can stay where they are as you conclude this section by saying, "Sometimes, people struggle to be responsible for their actions because they get caught up in making excuses for their behavior or blaming others. The voice in their head might tell them, 'That's not my fault, it's their fault. I'm not a bad person, so it can't be my fault.' This is when it's so important to remember that we all make mistakes. Part of being a kind and caring person is owning up to our missteps. Making excuses and naming reasons why the *other person* shouldn't be so upset isn't part of being responsible for your actions and isn't part of accountability. In our story, when Max said, 'What's the big deal? You can't expect to build a fort and not be prepared for a pillow fight,' he made excuses for his behavior and blamed Colline instead of being responsible for his part.

"Other times, people struggle to be responsible for their actions because their shame and feelings of unworthiness get in the way. The voice in their head might tell them, 'You can't do anything right, you're broken.' This is when it's so important to remember that we all make mistakes. Making a mistake doesn't make you bad. And focusing so much on how "bad" you are actually takes attention away from the person you hurt. This can make the pain for them worse because instead of you caring for them and their feelings, they can feel like they have to care for you and your feelings (even though you're not the one who was hurt). Shaming yourself for your mistake isn't part of being accountable, even though sometimes it feels like it can be. In our story, when Max responded with 'Oh my gosh, I'm so sorry. I'm the worst. I wasn't thinking. You probably never want to hang out with me again. I'm such a bad friend,' his shame and feelings of unworthiness got in the way of him being responsible for his actions."

Step 5   Practice

"Because saying a genuine 'I'm sorry' or a heartfelt 'I know I messed up,' can be really challenging, we're going to practice getting comfortable with these phrases."

In this activity, students will need an open area of the room. There will be three rounds. Instruct students to move around the space while making eye contact with each other. When you ring a bell (or call out the word *here*), students will pause in front of someone and do the following:

- **Round 1:** Say a genuine "I'm sorry" and then continue walking around until you ring the bell again.

- **Round 2:** Say a genuine "I'm sorry, I messed up" and then continue walking around until you ring the bell again.

- **Round 3:** Take a deep breath followed by "I'm sorry. I'm going to work on that" and then continue walking around until you ring the bell again.

Students should have a chance to interact with several people in the first two rounds and a few people in the last round.

CLASSROOM MANAGEMENT TIP:

During this activity, it's common to have students try to make a joke out of it or find a way to not take it seriously. To help reduce the chances of this happening, say the following as you introduce this activity: "This can feel awkward and uncomfortable. Oftentimes, if someone is laughing during this activity or not able to take it seriously, it's because they're embarrassed. It's okay to be embarrassed. See what you can do to overcome that embarrassment."

This is true, and it also primes students to interpret other students' laughter as embarrassment rather than a sense of being "too cool" to participate. Laughing unintentionally in this activity is totally okay! If you have students who are intentionally disrupting, you can kindly ask those students to sit quietly and wait for the activity to be done. Watching is still a form of participation.

After you end the last round, invite students back to their seats.

DISCUSSION QUESTIONS:

- What was that activity like? How did it feel? What did you notice?
  - *Talking points:* There's no right answer, but students will likely say it felt awkward. This is a great time to reinforce that being accountable and practicing consent, in general, can feel awkward. But avoiding feelings of awkwardness isn't a good reason not to be accountable and practice consent.

- Does taking responsibility feel easy or hard?
  - *Talking points:* Ask students to reflect on their real-life experiences or their experience of this activity. Share a personal experience of taking responsibility even though it was hard.

- How does it feel to hear someone be responsible for their actions?
  - *Talking points:* Again, ask students to reflect on their real-life experiences or their experience of this activity. Share a personal experience of having someone be responsible for their actions and how that felt for you.

Step 6   Discussion

"For the last part of this lesson, we're going to discuss what you can do when accountability doesn't go smoothly."

DISCUSSION QUESTIONS:

- What can you do if you don't get the accountability you need? Or if someone is not taking responsibility for their actions?
  - *Talking points:* Ask for it directly (verbally or in a letter), look to a teacher or trusted adult for support, or give them time.

- What are some ways you can approach someone to tell them you need accountability?

  - *Talking points:* Think about where and when you're approaching them. If you're looking for a quick "I'm sorry," you might just ask them to say sorry. If you need a longer conversation, try to find a private time to talk with them. Use "I" statements and be clear that you're asking them for accountability because you want to move past the hurt and continue a friendship with them.

- What can you do if you ask someone to be accountable and they won't be?

  - *Talking points:* Sometimes, no matter how much we would like an apology or accountability, we won't get it. We don't get to choose what other people say or do. That can be really hard. At times like this, we can turn to our friends for support and reassurance that what we are feeling makes sense and that we are strong enough to move through these hard feelings.

- What can you do if you apologize but the other person doesn't accept it?

  - *Talking points:* You might ask them what else you can do or if they need more time. You can talk to a teacher or trusted adult to help you navigate the situation. This is also when it's important to think about how apologies are only one form of accountability. We can't make people receive an apology. But we can still be accountable by reflecting on what happened and how we can do better in all of our relationships in the future. There are ways we can engage in accountability without anyone else's involvement.

Supporting This Lesson in Your Classroom's Culture

Model It

- Be accountable and take responsibility for your mistakes.

  - When you work with kids, you have the incredible opportunity to break the zero-sum myth. So easily, people can fall into believing "If you're right, I'm wrong" and "If I'm right, you're wrong." However, when conflict arises and we demonstrate that it's not about who's right and who's wrong, but about where each person lost their way, we teach kids that taking responsibility for our actions is doable and that admitting to mistakes doesn't make us bad people. By showing students that you can recognize where you messed up, you show them that it's okay for them to recognize where they mess up too.

- ○ When you call a student by a name they don't like, instead of saying "You can't expect me to remember everything," you can say "I'm sorry. I forgot. I'll work to remember for next time." When you zip a student's backpack up without their permission, instead of saying "I was just trying to help," you can say "Whoops, you want to do it yourself. If you need help, I'm here." When you raise your voice because you're frustrated, instead of saying "You keep asking me the same question, so what do you expect?" you can say "That didn't land right. I was frustrated and it got the best of me. Can I try again?" Even in moments where you feel like they were more in the wrong than you, you can still tend to your actions, model accountability, and show how to be responsible for your actions.

Coach It

- • Pay attention to "I'm sorry" box-checking.

  - ○ When you observe a student do something hurtful (e.g., taking a toy without asking, calling someone a mean name), it can be instinctive to tell that student to say sorry. But it's important to encourage accountability, not just apologies, and not just one form of apology. We need to be careful not to turn saying "I'm sorry" into a box a child has to check. "I'm sorry" is only one way to apologize, and an apology is only one part of accountability.

  - ○ Next time you encounter a situation where an apology or accountability is needed, consider using these questions to guide the student who misstepped into making amends:

    - – What do notice about their body language?

    - – What do you think they might be feeling?

    - – Why do you think they're feeling that way?

    - – What might help them feel better in this moment? Have you tried asking them what might help in this moment?

    - – Have you tried saying sorry? If you say sorry to them, what would you be sorry for?

    These questions can help the student better understand the impact of their actions and find a way to be accountable that is self-driven and feels genuine to them.

- This all being said, it's important to consider when box-checking might be enough. The conversation starters just listed can help only when a student is regulated enough to engage in the process thoughtfully. In the midst of conflict, a student will likely feel ashamed or defensive. Depending on how big those feelings are, conversations like this might not be feasible. In these moments, it might be strategic to settle for a surface-level apology, make some form of the apology yourself, or even move away from the topic of apology. This can look like:

  - A student mumbles, "Fine, I'm sorry." You respond, "Thank you for saying that." Later, have a conversation with this student about what, if anything, still needs to happen.

  - You (somewhat facetiously) say, "And this is where ideally, [Student's name] would say 'I'm sorry.' Since that's not where we're at right now, we'll circle back to this later."

  - You say, "It looks like [Student's name] isn't ready to give an apology quite yet. Let's come back to this later."

- If a student is too dysregulated to have a deeper conversation, it's okay to do just enough to get the class back on okay-enough terms. It can be tempting to want to get it right immediately. Remind yourself that now is not always the right time. You can share this with the student who was impacted by the misstep, too. Validate their hard feelings. Let them know you will come back to this when the other student has had time to settle, and then don't forget to circle back. With the student who caused hurt, you can talk to them about why they did what they did, what they can do next time, and whether an apology note or saying "I'm sorry" now makes sense.

Worksheet 5.4.1

Here are the four parts of accountability (Mingus, 2019):

1. **Self-reflection:** Ask yourself: What harm did my actions cause? How can I do better next time?

2. **Apologizing:** Say sorry and acknowledge the role you played in someone else's hurt.

3. **Repair:** Rebuild trust. Depending on your relationship, repair might take more time and effort or less time and effort.

4. **Behavior change:** Continue to reflect on what got in the way and make a commitment to not repeat the same behavior. You may even put systems in place so the same thing is less likely to happen again.

Directions: Review each of the actions listed here. Circle the actions that show accountability *or* might help mend the situation or the relationship. Place an X on top of the actions that don't show accountability *or* might hurt the person or relationship even more.

1. Say "I'm sorry."

2. Tell them, "What I did is not a big deal."

3. Think about what got in the way of your ability to use better consent skills.

4. Insist that they're overreacting.

5. Acknowledge how your actions (or inactions) had a negative impact or led to harm.

6. Blame yourself and label yourself a horrible person.

7. Remind yourself that consent is a practice and you're working on it.

8. Focus on what they need to feel safe and okay.

9. Ask them if they need space.

10. Don't say anything. Pretend nothing happened.

11. Tell them it's not your fault.

12. Let them know you're going to try harder to use your skills next time.

13. Listen to how they're feeling.

MODULE 6

Wrap-Up

LESSON 6.1

Putting It All Together

Learning Objectives:

By the end of this lesson, students will be able to:

1. Describe how to know whether they are practicing consent.

2. Describe the skills that support a consent practice.

3. Identify which consent skills they feel more competent in and which ones require more effort and work.

4. Describe their plan for continued consent practice.

Materials:

- Worksheet 6.6.1

Before You Start:

- Read through the lesson plan.

- Print worksheet 6.1.1 (one per student).

Time: 20 minutes

Step 1   **Introduce the Topic**

Guide the class in taking two deep breaths.

"We've reached the final lesson in this curriculum. We're going to review what we've learned about consent so far, celebrate our efforts in this journey, and talk about how we can continue learning and growing in our friendship skills and consent practices."

Step 2   **Discussion**

Ask students, "After all of these conversations about practicing consent and navigating desires and boundaries, how can a person know if they're actually practicing consent?"

As students answer, keep the following in mind: There is no correct answer to this question. Because we can't mind-read, it's impossible to know for sure if you're asking enough, checking in as needed, and noticing enough nonverbal cues in any given moment. But practicing consent isn't about getting it right 100 percent of the time.

It's about doing our part to uplift our desires and the other person's desires, and to be a guardian of your boundaries and their boundaries. A student of mine once answered this question with "I feel like practicing consent is about paying attention." Of course, we need to do more than just pay attention, but in order to practice consent in the way a moment calls for, paying attention is foundational.

Then remind students of the following analogy:

"Consent is a practice like kindness is a practice. If I want to talk to you and I ask, 'Can we please talk?' I am being kind by saying please. But I don't get to just label that entire interaction as kind. Practicing kindness in this situation also means listening, not interrupting, and being thoughtful about my words and my volume. Now, if I accidentally raise my voice during this conversation with you, it doesn't mean I am an unkind or mean person. It means I made a mistake. I can apologize, be accountable, and reset. Kindness is an ongoing practice. I'm working to pay attention to myself and to them.

"Beyond this, I don't get to mark the interaction as 'kind' all on my own. I need to consider how the other person felt. Did they feel like I was practicing kindness? Is there a way I could have been kinder from their point of view? Just like we talk about how to do our best to practice kindness, through this learning, we're going to talk about how to do our best to practice consent."

Step 3 Discussion Continued

"Another way we can think about the practice of consent is by comparing it to sports." Ask students to raise their hand if they play a sport and invite them to share what sport they play.

Pick a sport that students have named and, from there, form an analogy. I've used basketball as an example. You can use basketball for this analogy or create your own using the details of another sport.

Ask students the following questions:

- What skills does a person need to know to be good at basketball?

  - *Talking points:* Dribbling, shooting, and passing are the main ones.

- Is it enough to know the instructions for dribbling a basketball, or do you need to actually take the time to do the activity?

  - *Talking points:* You need to actually practice doing the activity. Knowing how to place your hand on the ball and knowing that you're supposed to look up doesn't mean that you can dribble the ball while looking up in the way you'll need to.

- If you learn the instructions for dribbling, try to dribble, and fumble the ball, does that mean you'll never be good at basketball?
  - *Talking points:* No, getting good at anything takes time!
- How do you get better at basketball?
  - *Talking points:* By practicing, getting coached, not comparing yourself to others, and working on the aspects of it that don't come naturally to you.
- If you want to play a game of basketball, is it possible for a person tell you exactly what you need to do to in order to be successful?
  - *Talking points:* No, each game is going to be different. What you do will depend on many variables and possibilities, including how you're feeling that day, who is on your team, how your teammates are doing, where you are playing, who is on the other team, and what their skills are.
- If you make a mistake in a basketball game, should you just stop playing?
  - *Talking points:* One mistake, or even many mistakes, doesn't mean the game or your basketball career is over. The same is true for consent. You do your best, you practice, and when you mess up, you take a deep breath and call on your skills to see if you can make things better. Then, outside of the game or the situation, you can consider how the mistake happened and work on your skills in that area.

"In basketball, just like in consent, we do our best to learn the skills, think critically, and practice often so we have the skills ready at our fingertips. This way, we can be as prepared as possible for any situation."

Step 4   Activity

"Now, let's take time to reflect on what it means to have a consent practice."

Introduce worksheet 6.1.1 to the class and review the instructions. Give students about six minutes to complete the worksheet. Let students know that this worksheet is for their eyes only. Once students are done, see if there are any comments or questions.

Step 5 Conclusion

Reinforce for students that we need to keep up our skills. Professional NBA basketball players have scheduled practice all the time to keep their skills sharp. We need to do the same. Let students know that you will be returning to some of these activities and learnings in the future (and then remember to do so!).

Thank the class for their participation and lead them in a round of applause for all of the learning and work they've done.

Supporting This Lesson in Your Classroom's Culture

From here, it's all about continued reflection and practice.

The only way to learn is to try. In supporting students in their consent practice, you will mess up, you will wish you handled something differently, and you will struggle in figuring out what you "should" do. Pay attention to yourself and to others. If you are taking the time to internalize these lessons and ideas, you're doing great! Modeling and coaching these lessons will get easier the more you do them. Deep breaths and many high-fives from me! You got this!

Worksheet 6.1.1

Directions: Answer the following questions to reflect on what it means to have a consent practice.

1. What skills support a strong consent practice? Think about the skills we've learned in this curriculum.

2. If you fumble in your consent practice, what might that mean?

3. What can you do to get stronger in your own consent practice?

4. How can you help others get better in their consent practice?

Additional Resources

Child Sexual Abuse Prevention: Resources for Teachers and Students

- **The Bayar Group:** https://www.thebayargroup.com

- **Consent Parenting:** https://www.consentparenting.com

- **Darkness to Light:** https://www.d2l.org

- **Educate2Empower Publishing:** https://e2epublishing.info

- **Parenting Safe Children:** https://parentingsafechildren.com

Power and Identity: Lesson Plans

- **Crip Camp Curriculum:** https://cripcamp.com/curriculum

- **Institute for Humane Education:** https://humaneeducation.org/lesson-plans-curricula

- **Learning for Justice:** https://www.learningforjustice.org/classroom-resources/lessons

References

....

For your convenience, the exercises in this book are available
for download at **www.pesipubs.com/kidsconsent**

Baczynski, M., & Scott, E. (2022). *Creating consent culture: A handbook for educators.* Jessica Kingsley
Publishers.

Harrison, D. L. (Guest). (2020, June 8). Solutions not punishment collaborative with Da'Shaun
Harrison (Bonus) [Audio podcast episode]. In *Sex Ed with DB.* https://soundcloud.com
/user-260204496/solutions-not-punishment

Hirsch, J. S., Khan, S. R., Wamboldt, A., & Mellins, C. A. (2019). Social dimensions of sexual consent
among cisgender heterosexual college students: Insights from ethnographic research. *Journal of
Adolescent Health, 64*(1), 26–35. https://doi.org/10.1016/j.jadohealth.2018.06.011

Lockwood Harris, K. (2018). Yes means yes and no means no, but both these mantras need to
go: Communication myths in consent education and anti-rape activism. *Journal of Applied
Communication Research, 46*(2), 155–178. https://doi.org/10.1080/00909882.2018.1435900

Martin, B., & Dalzen, R. (2021). *The art of receiving and giving: The wheel of consent.* Luminare Press.

Mingus, M. (2019, December 12). The four parts of accountability & how to give a genuine apology.
Leaving Evidence. https://leavingevidence.wordpress.com/2019/12/18/how-to-give-a-good-apology
-part-1-the-four-parts-of-accountability

Pound, P., Denford, S., Shucksmith, J., Tanton, C., Johnson, A. M., Owen, J., & Campbell, R.
(2017). What is best practice in sex and relationship education? A synthesis of evidence, including
stakeholders' views. *BMJ Open, 7*(5), e014791. https://doi.org/10.1136/bmjopen-2016-014791

Setty, E. (2020). Sex and consent in contemporary youth sexual culture: The 'ideals' and the 'realities.'
Sex Education, 21(3), 331–346. https://doi.org/10.1080/14681811.2020.1802242

Silverstein, S. (1964). *The giving tree.* HarperCollins.

Acknowledgments

Thank you to everyone at PESI who has helped to make this book a reality.

Kate Sample read my DIY workbook and saw its potential as a classroom-focused curriculum. Dr. Jenessa Jackson and Karsyn Morse helped me refine my ideas so that teachers everywhere would be able to feel confident in facilitating them.

Betty Martin, creator of the Wheel of Consent®, and Robyn Dalzen, co-founder of the School of Consent, have fundamentally changed the way I understand relationships and the meaning of integrity, and how I want to show up as a teacher. My gratitude for their work is boundless.

If we want to create meaningful change, we need to follow the science. I'm thankful for the researchers in sociology, psychology, education, and philosophy who have examined the impact of SEL, the effectiveness of sexual violence interventions, and the way we understand consent and our obligations to each other.

Throughout the book-writing process—and always—Ella Dorval Hall and Colline Laninga have been by my side. I don't know if I believe in soul mates, but I know I have soul friends.

My parents have always loved me and believed in me, offering the roots and wings that have enabled me to discover my true self.

Lastly, I'm grateful for the teachers, practitioners, and parents who embody kindness, compassion, and equity so that our young people will grow up to do the same.

About the Author

Sarah Casper is the founder of Comprehensive Consent, a social-emotional learning approach to equipping kids and teens with the knowledge and skills necessary for healthy, respectful, and joyful relationships. As a former children's yoga teacher and PsyD candidate, Sarah incorporates research and practices from mindfulness and psychology to help strengthen students' abilities to navigate their inner and outer worlds with thoughtfulness, curiosity, and care. Through her in-school workshops, online classes, and social media content, Sarah has helped thousands of kids, adolescents, and adults throughout the world shift their understanding of consent as something we simply "give" and "get" to a practice we are all responsible to uphold. You can find her on Instagram @ComprehensiveConsent.